Believership

The Superpower Beyond Leadership

(Volume 1: The Experience)

Mike Vacanti

No part of this publication may be reproduced, stored in a retrieval system, or transmitted, in any form or by any means, electronic, mechanical, photocopying, recording, or otherwise, without the written permission of the author.

First published by Dog Ear Publishing
8888 Keystone Crossing
Suite 1300
Indianapolis, IN 46240
www.dogearpublishing.net

ISBN: 978-145757-127-5

This book is printed on acid-free paper.
Printed in the United States of America

To my wife, Sue, whom may not have selected this wild journey, yet has been my guide throughout. And to my 5 adult kids, who have inspired me to learn and grow every day.

Introduction:

The Journey to Believership

I was transitioning from Seattle to Minneapolis after a two-year stint doing my fifth merger and acquisition integration. Turmoil wasn't new to me. Actually, I kind of thrived in this environment. Yet this time, it felt more like hanging in limbo than transitioning – being stuck rather than moving forward.

As the "chaos-pilot," the integrator during a M&A, that role disappears after a period of time as the business settles into the next phase, the plan evolves, the new realities set in, change happens, and continuation requires adopting a new position along the journey. As before, I didn't fit into the operational state of the business. "Business as usual" just isn't me.

Felling stuck was new and uncomfortable. Seeking the next adventure, I was engaged in long courting processes with two companies; one in Minneapolis and one in Seattle, and many more exploratory conversations. Each of the two opportunities-in-courtship were with long standing entrepreneurial entities looking for acceleration and expansion. However, as often is the case, the owners knew they needed someone different, but couldn't let go of the internal desire to find someone the same as them, an extension of themselves. Neither made the decision.

During these three months, I was succumbing to the turmoil. Where do I go from here? Doubt, confusion, questioning everything from values, beliefs, my history, my future, my relationships… everything. It was a downward spiral that pushed me into escape. That feeling of despair was seriously messing with my head, as I contemplated where I belonged. Where was "home" for me geographically, professionally, and psychologically? What was churning deep inside was urging me to walk away from the bulk of my life's work, even if it alienated me from family and close relationships, the very foundation that gives my life meaning. I just wanted to go somewhere alone and start over.

Existing in an unhappy state is misery, and I was miserable. I felt like everything happening to me was out of my control. I was reacting to circumstance. My innate strengths - the ability to create, my open-mindedness, my optimism – were weakening. Without realizing it, I was becoming closed-minded, and as I focused on the pressures from the outside, I was losing the power from the inside. Hope fought despair. Fear and doubt battled love. and perspective became cloudy. It felt like the wind was out of my sails, the waves were violently swelling, and I could only see the darkening, thunderous sky as I drifted further from shore. My navigation system was broken. I was becoming smaller, living in the challenge, and losing sight of what was most important; relationships, family, friends and the potential for future impact. I lacked vision – I lost my gratitude.

The time came for me to let go of the Seattle apartment, sell or donate all its contents and pack only personal belongs into my car for the "move" back to my house and home in Minneapolis. That long drive was a metaphor for the journey ahead.

Wake up, Mike. Get up and move. Your grasping at the past. Not seeing possibilities. I am not a victim. I persevere, I am resilient, I have a great life. I have a wonderful wife and adult children who are good human beings, show up with a growth mindset, treat people well and contribute with belief and ambition. Time to climb back and enjoy this next season – start a new journey.

My son, Michael (Mike Vacanti, Jr.) was home visiting from Manhattan, after stepping away from a two-year stint training Gary Vaynerchuk, and building his strength and fitness business. Apparently seeing me in in this state-of-being, was disturbing, so he said let's take a walk. The gift he offered aided my new path. He said, Dad, you don't care about nutrition, don't exercise and it gets worse from here if you continue in this pattern. He offered to stick around for 2-3 months and "get me going" on the journey to better health. I said yes, and thank you, knowing there was room for improvement, but skeptical of lasting change. Nine months later I was back at my college-athletic playing weight, and have maintained while continuing to build strength for 2 years. My limiting beliefs, accepted restrictions based on past patterns of behavior, were shattered and swept aside. His belief in me, ignited my belief. When your kid offers a gift of love, you start to re-examine what really matters. This elevated my belief in positive change. For me, it solidified that Believership starts from the inside and begins with ourselves.

I put three tenets in place for myself:

1) Stop self-sabotaging

2) Have a plan

3) Smile

Stop self-sabotaging was a deep reflection of my core beliefs that were informing my behaviors and actions, and creating the perspective. The goal was to discard the limiting beliefs, double-down on the intentional, selected core and align my behaviors. This allowed me to create my circumstances from the inside out, not react to the outside stimulus and perspectives.

The first step in the plan was to hire a coach and do a deep dive into my professional experiences. I had been asked in an interview, "you have these 5 different mergers/acquisitions where your team achieved phenomenal results, why is that?" To which I summoned my one-octave lower, "business" voice and gave my best business-jargon answer. As I walked out, I realized I didn't really know, I only assumed from my own uninformed perspective. My now friend, Kathleen Crandall, took me through her deep discovery process. Kathy asked me the profound question, which is the backbone of her process, "What happens because of you^{TM}?."

This extremely comprehensive program walked me through personal introspection along with a thick packet of feedback solicitation from former bosses, employees, clients, partners and even friends, exploring how they experienced me through these adventures. It was a ton of data that offered a full picture of how I showed up, my strengths, weaknesses and uniqueness. All of me, flaws and features, good and bad. As we walked to our cars following one of last meetings together, Kathy asked, "so what's going to happen now?" I quipped, "I'm going to bring the word love into the business world."

From this work, the powerful understanding of leadership emerged. I named it "Believership". Believership best describes "what happened because of me" in my leadership experiences, where I was leading teams through transformation and navigating the fear and doubt of chaos during periods of great change. It was the active ingredient and outcome for each individual, uniquely for them personally, and strong enough to hold everyone together as a unit, with a unified objective. We each found our self-belief in the strength of each other, which compounded our contribution to the whole. We believed in ourselves, we believed we could succeed, believed in the foreseeable mission and in possibilities for the future. Each of us, individually and together, through these experiences came to understand the power, the availability and the choice, to embrace the impact of Believership.

Believership is the Superpower Beyond Leadership. It lives inside each of us beckoning to be released. It has transformative implications for our lives and those around us as we ignite the power within, resisting the constraints forced upon us by limiting definitions of leadership, suppressed beliefs, and narrow, historic perspectives. With Believership, we experience the power of possibility for a brighter future of business. It busts the doors open for diversity and inclusion, relies on the intuitive ability to navigate through continuous change, fuel innovation, and lift others onto the journey with us. It belongs to everyone.

The next step of the "plan" was creating a high-achieving team program based on the learnings from consulting work, when a client asked me to condense the work we had done, using the "Believership" principles, into a 1-day workshop so they could get me in front of more teams. I took that program to companies across the country for a year and from this work, and the network that emerged because of it, a true purpose emerged – The HumansFirst Club event series, which has turned into a global movement with thousands of contributing "members" and growing consortium of extraordinary "presenting members," who are each game-changing, high-impact voices leading the shift to a brighter future. "Smile." Number three on the list, number one in importance, was simply to start each day with gratitude. Grounded in the creative, expansive wonder and bounty of my journey, and sharing these gifts out to every person I engage through each day, became my center of gravity. It took some practice.

I committed to sharing this experience of discovering 'the superpower beyond leadership' as an expression of possibilities, and to open dialog. I invite you to explore the hope I gained through the continuously experienced belief that *given the opportunity, people will amaze us.*

This is Volume 1: The Experience. It's the starting point for a journey we will take together, you and me, and the many who are influencing my extraordinary personal growth every day. Through this expansive discovery of other's journeys and the implementation of the Believership principles, 'Volume 2: The Discovery' will follow in a short time. 'Volume 3: The Outcomes,' will follow that.

I hope you will join this adventure and offer your voice, your experiences to the conversation.

Chapter 1:

What Happened To All These People

At fourteen years old, I started spending my summers in my Dad's manufacturing plant. I packed my lunch and punched my card into the time-clock slot promptly at 7:30, punched out at lunch, in at 12:30 and again at day's end. Factory work at 14 was met with some typical teenage rumbling and complaining, but I had the flexibility to get to baseball, football or hockey practice. Having some cash put away for the school year was a bit of freedom as well.

Work was a good thing. While summer months in a non-air-conditioned warehouse could get a bit stifling, I liked what we were doing and the ability to tinker, make stuff and learn the business. We made protective athletic equipment for hockey and football. As the years went on, I was well versed in plastic molding, foam density, anatomy and body composition, the physics of impact, as well as multiple materials from cloth to leather to nylon and became a decent sewer. But what I really loved was interacting with people. Through college I had the opportunity to engage in trade shows, sales calls, demonstrations, and the operational facets of material management, order flow, pricing, finance and marketing.

After taking a shot at playing hockey beyond college, I was eager to become fully immersed in the business and believed my "career" was set - doing what I loved; what was most natural. We had 52 reps operating throughout the US and Canada. I was a product expert - I made the stuff, and was also a former athlete with many beneficial relationships in sports, and a love of people. Traveling 85% of the time was fun. Team to team, city to city, rep to rep and multiple sporting-goods store visits in every city. As well as getting professional and college teams and players to wear the gear.

In that environment, at that time, it was absolutely essential to show up as your genuine self, or you're out. These independent store owners, buyers, pro athletes, and institutional equipment managers could sniff out a corporate puke in a heartbeat and shut you down. They had seen it all, had plenty of choice, and had no tolerance for posturing. I had to know my stuff, talk straight, understand and care about their business and the velocity of goods moving through the store. Daily profit was their livelihood.

Sure, I read books and attended some training set up by a board-member and exec at 3M, and was learning every day. But fundamentally, success was dependent on how I showed up, who I was; open, flawed, knowledgeable and honest. If they didn't want to hang out with me - I didn't get their business.

The company went public and grew. Momentum was building, shares were accumulating value, these were good times, but lessons lied ahead. To further our reach, expand the sales and distribution channels, accelerate growth and provide year-round cash flow, we acquired a successful softball/baseball company. The complex, board-led transaction hit some bumps and started to unravel. The next year was an education in proxy battles, lawsuits and court proceedings. The complexity of business structure, and psychology of people in business was on full display. Lessons are learned through adversity, pressure and turmoil. These were lessons never taught in business school.

At 29, I walked away from the whole industry. Not wanting to jump off the family business wagon and play a role with another company in the industry, I decided marketing and advertising were best aligned with my creative business passion. So, I reinvented. It was a crazy leap and many people were clear to tell me: "You don't have the background for this;" and "your too old to make this move;" or "this isn't for entrepreneurs." Some of this was true, some narrow perspective, but overall, people were sincere about helping, and I was committed. In six weeks, I talked to 14 executives for "informational interviews" and a bunch of account execs, creative directors, and others associated with various media and print production. It finally happened. I was hired.

Financially it was a step backward, the company car was gone, replaced with an old Volvo that I could repair on my own with a manual in hand, yet it was exciting to be on a steep learning curve. What stood out the most for me, and carried me forward was the critical lessons and experiences of the past; *Business is People - People are Business.*

A couple years later and I was back in sports through the advertising lens running the account for the local professional sports franchise. This path led to other relationships, interests and opportunities and for the next decade, I operated my own marketing company, anchored by my patented automotive child safety product, raising my 5 young kids, coaching high school and youth sports. Nothing like that 30-something energy!

I was now an inventor, advertising, merchandising, marketing, manufacturing and sales guy. From a traditional career standpoint, my resume would have been an irrecoverable mess, had I ever needed to create one, which to this point, I hadn't.

The mid-nineties were an explosive time of innovation, as the power of the Internet took hold. Money was flowing into technology and business concepts with fervor. New companies were born, e-commerce was a new threat and opportunity, mobile phones were proliferating, downloading, file sharing and other expansive concepts were in play. It was alluring and I was on the outside. Certainly, there was a ton of marketing opportunity, but I was not in the arena, and the storm was pulling me in.

Then the opportunity came. A client needed help pulling together a major pitch for Target Corp, to use an early stage voice and file system to enable schools and teachers to better communicate with students, parents and each other. Learning the technology and its application in this environment was exciting, and the offer was timely and compelling. The deal got done. Through this process, it also became conceptually possible to extend the core technology and launch a unified message platform, linking mobile and land-line phones to the internet, allowing voice and email to interface - voicemail to email and email to voicemail, along with other file sharing from phone infrastructure to internet protocol.

We re-purposed the client pitch, raised some venture capital and suddenly an internet startup was launched. Another new adventure, another new skill. The next year was wild, meeting with major telco and mobile phone companies, industry groups, venture firms, and grabbing center stage at trade shows, conferences and media outlets. It was about technology, it was about a new and exciting service platform, and the possibilities of the future of business. It was very complex, conceptual and required a lot of business chops, yet as always, it was about relationships with people and possibilities through connection.

When the "internet-bubble" burst around 2000, many companies were stuck 'holding the bag' on tech acquisitions that were no longer the venture-cash draws they had been during the boom. Businesses were crashing at an alarming rate as the support funding dried up. The fate of Bridgecom.com, our unified communications platform, fell in the wreckage.

Through one of the investor groups, and a friend in the executive placement business, I landed at a publicly traded firm that was holding an acquired tech company that was no longer an investment magnet but an albatross and an ill-fitting burden. It was a great opportunity to work the magic of partnership, re-platform the core technology, build an active revenue base and then sell it as market vertical to the content management platform company, that later sold to Oracle.

This was fun and rewarding. I craved more of these experiences. Through a partnership where we were doing due-diligence on potential deals, I took on a project to help a tech-staffing firm, buy and integrate a solutions-based tech integrator and custom development shop and stuck around for the first year of integration.

Stepping Inside the Corporate World

After a year of that, I suddenly found myself in a situation that required a resume for the first time in my 2-decade career. I was recruited by a friend to another struggling tech services company that had lost over half its value, loaded with debt and in the evaluation process of being acquired by a huge multinational, Japanese-based firm. I went all in.

The acquisition happened rapidly, immediately followed by two additional acquisitions. An ambitious 4-company/4-culture roll up was in full swing. I was 40 years old, and for the first time in my career I was part of a company with an HR team, and the accompaniment of ceremonial business orchestration mandates in every process for every operating unit. As a VP with P&L responsibility it was on me to comply, train and deliver the corporate mandates to the large, complex and multi-location teams, bring exceptional value and project satisfaction to clients, and manage the partnership with Microsoft.

At the beginning, plans and people were coming together. It was chaotic with constant, sometimes sweeping changes occurring regularly, causing continuous doubt and trepidation among the newly mashed-up teams, but we were getting it done and delivering to clients and growing revenue. The anticipation of contributing alongside this world-class combination of talent, knowledge and leadership was exciting. There was seriously deep and rich talent in this combined group, including some of the best leaders I've experienced in all my years. Many lifelong friendships were developed, and are valued still today. Potential was very high, there was good reason to believe and commit. Then the leadership shifted direction, and what appeared to be a conglomeration of incredible people and possibilities started unraveling.

The most senior leaders needed to flex their authority and push out nonconforming ideals, and challenging perspectives. The good leaders were minimized or discarded, while the others battled for power and control. With poor leadership, poor behavior is rampant. Under the pressure of the intellectually inflexible. Command-with-power executives put no value on teams, it was more like throwing people together in a cage match. Hierarchy was the golden rule. The further up you were, the worse you could treat people. Posturing, leveraging, political agendas, climbing over each other, secret alliances — it was like an adult version of middle school.

These were proven, experienced leaders, and they were failing miserably. It was easy to forecast that the anticipated value-multiplier of the acquisitions, was not sustainable. The hierarchal, authoritative leadership structure was solidly in place, but there was little belief in the future, the vision and modeling from leadership, or the ability elevate the whole and take good care of the highly talented teams. The equation was set on division rather than multiplication, negative charge, not positive charge, and therefore, it was time for me step away. I had lost my belief.

For decades, my experiences, what I had learned (not been taught), established an ideal for what business is, and can be. I acted on these ideas in my approach to people, business, innovation, and leadership through the extraordinary diverse experiences. It was highly successful. This situation made me realize I had a strong belief and an uncommon philosophy of how to engage – how to lead - by listening and owning the responsibility while sharing the authority; to inspire and allow others to find their belief, honor their perspective, and their timeline. These previous leader's approach to business, their way of command and control leadership, was way out of alignment with my mental models, my belief in people, and constructs of organizational behavior and relationships with other humans.

Recognizing this great divide, became the wakeup call I needed to stay true to my beliefs, my experiences and not acquiesce to the "standard" models of exploitation, leverage over others and callous maximization — extracting value rather than creating value. Stepping away was an emancipating decision, and set the cornerstone for the work I do, and how I live my life today.

The leadership's authority and power were clear, but very few believed in them or their vision for the business. Surely this is not how the majority of companies, the majority of people operate - is it? Experiencing these behaviors had me wondering...

What happen to all these people?

Who taught them to battle every situation in a 'zero-sum' game? Why did they stop thinking, surrender their beliefs, and assimilate so readily? Where did their creativity and curiosity go? The environment, the culture inside the company was unlike the experiences and people I had engaged over the past 20 years. Or, perhaps I had only assumed it wasn't, because I looked at each person, each experience through the lens of my relationships, endeavors and ambitions; a reflection of myself.

Of the 5 mergers and acquisitions I experienced, only 2 of the leadership teams remained in place for more than 3 years; one remains today. So many lives were impacted, hardships endured all for the gain of a few, while creating more harm than good for the individuals, the clients and economies in the markets of operation. Their impact on the business was fleeting. Their impact on all the people subject to their incompetent bravado was significant and detrimental.

Over the years as I've watched others, in different but similar structures, and pondered "what happened?" I have formed a very plausible and proven thesis: As their careers progressed and they climbed the ladder, little pieces of themselves were chipped away from the inside. Each new role, responsibility and manager caused capitulation to continue along the trajectory. By the time they were in a leadership role, their insides were darkened, they were hardly recognizable as humans.

Chapter 2:

Leadership Is Not Enough

We have a leadership crisis.

Experiencing the dynamics and chaos of mergers and acquisitions five times, provides a great lens for people-watching. At times it felt like I was transported back to that little kid walking through the mass of 200,000 people per day wondering the cramped Minnesota State Fairgrounds, gawking at the flowing sea of people, each unfiltered outburst of group and family drama, and the oddity of each of us individually. Aside from the dizzying overindulgence of everything-fried-on-a-stick, getting tossed around like a marble in a blender on the midway rides, and uncertain if I was inside or outside of the carnival-show at times, it was an amazing wonder of humanity. Just like jumping into the circus of ideas and egos clashing when upheaval us underway in a corporate setting. There was little distinction in behavior from top to bottom.

It was clear to see who was who from a personality and belief standpoint, making it easy to envision how things would play out based on the individual, the environment how they related to others. It was predictable because of the behaviors and decision patterns, and the mindset of the leaders. How they got there was who they were.

With Greater Awareness Comes Greater Choice

Today's prevailing and failing management theory drags us through history, and is excruciatingly screaming for change.

Through the past century, we've experienced massive innovation, scientific and biological discovery and exponential information gains. The phones in our hands have a million-times more computing power than the IBM mainframe used by NASA to send men to the moon and back.

Our ability to understand the world has evolved in all areas of life, science and business. From deep space to ocean floor, to the tiniest cells in our bodies and floating particles we breathe, how our minds and bodies work, we have knowledge and choices as never before, including instantaneous access to global information previously requiring decades to amass only a small portion. It's a different world.

Although every area of life has been affected, has evolved to a new state, our approach to leadership remains rigidly beholden to the centuries-old model. Truly baffling!

We've sped past the repeatable, process-orchestration, algorithmic period of the past 30 years at an incredible pace, compared to the industrial eras of the century prior. Today we are awakening to the realities that we're in a whole new paradigm; a new era that is more complex, disruptive and very different from previous eras. Change is more significant and accelerating. We will see greater shifts in the next 5 years than *the previous twenty*.

As businesses race to catch up to this rapid transformation, we continue to force our limiting beliefs, behavior preference, our biases and burdens on people in the workplace, resisting the inevitable: Our belief in leadership models must change - now.

Who is a Leader?

From early century Mediterranean variances, through the enlightened Renaissance period, into the industrial era, leadership ideals and archetypes have contrasted, shifted and weaved in parallel; Stoic/Philosopher, Warrior/King, Innovator/Visionary, Governor/Uniter, and many more variations through time and geography. With thousands of written accounts and references, it's not hard to discover a definition.

The critically important challenge we face today is emancipating people and businesses from the predominant leadership model that has far exceeded it's time of relevance.

Over a century ago, Max Weber set the belief of bureaucracy in motion. Control people and costs will stay down, production will increase - the fundamental business formula. Frederick Taylor later expounded with "scientific management," which was like a fresh coat of paint on an old fence post, adding only rigor to the coating.

Eighty years later, Robert Greenleaf wrote a brilliant story about a servant who was a leader, proposing the elements of leadership in wide discussion today: listening, empathy, healing, awareness of others, situations and oneself, persuasion, conceptualization, foresight, stewardship, commitment to the growth of people, and building community. It's a phenomenally enlightened belief that was poorly executed and diluted over time, becoming a cliché.

Greenleaf's ideals however, spawned an industry unto itself. The people that have since built businesses around the story messed it up with their repackaging of Weberism (which is crazy), applying the theory that the "great-man" can now hoist the entire org from the bottom, inverting the pyramid of hierarchy, the status-quo, to change it. Of course, they took care to sprinkle in the "nice" words from the story. Later, as if all these "touchy-feel-y" concepts were too much to handle, the "institute" people compressed it into the word, "trust" and spawned a whole new industry. The clearest, most profound measure is offered by Greenleaf himself: "The best test, and difficult to administer, is this: Do those served grow as persons? Do they, while being served, become healthier, wiser, freer, more autonomous, more likely themselves to become servants?"

Deming and Drucker were the next prolific voices. I'm a fan of Peter Drucker's teachings on management. It's important to distinguish between leadership and management and Drucker's work helps create that distinction. He's an important figure in business evolution, perhaps the wise authority on management. I still have my "Daily Drucker" book of business wisdom. However, his writings on leadership fall way short. Merging of the two disciplines becomes a dissertation on authoritative control, forcing process, methods and analysis through the chain of command. Switching back and forth across the tracks of management and leadership, Drucker turned leadership into a meaningless synonym.

Deming focused on behaviors, and provides a clearer, more expandable vision. His work around Total Quality Management encompassed all operational areas and repeatable efficiencies in business, and he provided little guidance regarding the linkages between specific leadership styles and TQM behaviors or policies. He did not provide a definition for his conceptualization of leadership, with the understanding that there can be no single archetype, leaving room for all to become leaders. He moved the ball of evolution and landed a reasonable basis for philosophical change.

Although obvious and understood how flawed this is, Weber's detached machismo of hierarchy has been the standard model for over 120 years, and remains predominate today.

This model of leadership is a severely restrictive and a harmful limiting belief. Harmful to people bearing the brunt "down-stream" in the hierarchical pressure structure, and harmful to the business with a crippling inability to gain vision and adapt to change.

Weber's-world is the root of our modern leadership crisis, and continues to gain momentum, forcing itself against the grain of humanity and wisdom. We've coveted the dominate male, following history, it's the legend of men who conquer, modeled by the traits attributed to men of war. Power, control, battle. We covet the analytical over the creative, condemn the curious and reward the compliant.

We Want Change But Won't Change

Leadership is *the* problem today. And one we are reluctant to address. The need is obvious and alarming:

Today, over 80% of change-initiatives fail, costing >$1 Trillion, with more loses in productivity, yet a large majority of companies and executive management teams resist change and cling to the power of status quo.

120,000 unnecessary deaths each year are caused by toxic work environments. Your boss has a greater impact on your health than your doctor. This cultural and leadership crisis is costing $600 billion in additional healthcare; exceeding $1 trillion when considering lost time.

70% US, 85% global employees are disengaged with 25% of them actively trying to sink the boat.

The mental and physical health tolls are astounding and documented. The inability of corporations to adapt and change. Accelerating outside business model disruption. Exploding technology possibilities. 5 generations working together for the first time in history. And denial persists.

In 5 snippets of data above, a potential $2 trillion budget is on the table as incentive to fix the problem.

We don't have the solutions in place, we need to create them. And we cannot create them adhering to the non-creative models and patterns of the recent and distant past. It's simply preposterous that we continue down the same path, with the same institutional thinking, and our imperiling ideal of leadership.

The flaw of selection

The problem is exacerbated by continually forcing these prototypical containers of fabled traits and characteristics into our selection process, mimicking, accepting and perpetuating a broken model. Narrow patterns have been created, replicated and honed with determined rigor to filter through the identification of high-potentials and orchestrate their ascend up the ladder.

Examples of the wrong way, the wrong person, are exposed every day, often to the detriment of many inside and outside of the companies in their charge.

To have better leadership, we need to stop selecting and promoting the wrong people, those that fit the standard archetype. Instead, we can recognize that great leaders create Believership cultures, empowering all to act on their belief, allowing the best to rise. This is also the fundamental key to real and sustainable inclusion in leadership. Change the belief, allow the best to rise, and value character and capacity of the person, not an idyllic persona or imitation of someone else.

In his research-laden book, "Why Do So Many Incompetent Men Become Leaders?," Tomas Chamorro-Premuzic shares:

"The paradoxical implication is that the same psychological characteristics that enable male managers to rise to the top of the corporate or political ladder are actually responsible for their downfall. In other words, what it takes to *get* the job is not just different from, but also the reverse of, what it takes to *do the job well*. As a result, too many incompetent people are promoted to management jobs, and promoted over more competent people."

Organizations perpetuate the selection criteria and pass it on through time like a coveted treasure, adopted as a best-practice - unchecked and unchallenged. This archetypal view is a deep-rooted limiting belief holding back progress in a continuously stagnant loop.

We ask the wrong questions

Enjoying a guest appearance on John Eades, Transformational Leader podcast in Charlotte, NC one afternoon before the evening HumansFirst event, we discussed selecting and promoting the wrong people into leadership. He asked, "what is the one question you would ask a candidate to determine if they will be a good leader." Without hesitation, I said, "tell me about your relationships with the people you work with." The highest form of leadership is relationships; one to one, group to group with consistent presence. Without relationships, you're not really leading, you're managing or commanding.

To drop the rock on habitual error, we need to ask what Kathy Crandall guided me to explore when I created the Believership philosophy: What happens because of the leader (you)? Who they are as a human being is exceedingly more important than the position they held, or their management chops. Self-awareness, core beliefs and continuous growth in pursuit of being their best selves are critical keys. Character, capacity, and then skills. Skills are easy to learn. Capacity must be exercised, stretched and is variable person to person. Character is the core, both heart and brain intelligence, beliefs, relationships, and the sum of experiences.

Reaching backward, clinging to the Archetypes of leadership and continuing to drag them forward is harming people, blocking innovation and growth in business and excluding the potential of would be great leaders.

Great Leaders Know
That Leadership Alone Is Not Enough

Leadership is becoming increasingly more complicated and unpredictable in this transformational period. Transformation involves thinking differently. It cannot work top down - it must work throughout. Like the human body, all parts must be in sync, one body with many members. Little orchestration is needed when there is not a single dominant member. This allows natural coordination of every individual, every team, every unit, performing autonomously connected in a collective belief system, honoring natural dependencies. From the simplest function, like heart to brain, hand to mouth, to the spectacular display of athleticism, dance, and teamwork, we understand the natural magnificence of movement and imagination and performance. Decisions and accountability are inherent to the role of leadership, and operationally it becomes unified, expandable and sustainable through natural dependencies, not forced, structural orchestration.

We've managed to stomp out natural evolution through control, over orchestration and rigid compliance to a fear-based, carrot and stick mentality. The primary barrier to positive change is a leadership system that constrains and kills possibilities. We need to go deep into the mental data base, our belief systems, highlight this enormous container of "Prescriptive-Authority" and hit DELETE. Removing this barrier will allow the creation of a critically needed future model of leadership for this non-industrial era of significant, rapid and unchartered turbulence.

Until we change our minds, we cannot change business. Until we let go of the flawed perspective on leadership, we will exacerbate our leadership crisis.

Chapter 3:

Real But Not Seen

Leadership forges a path.
Believership is a paved road.

Taking a walk back through a long journey, trigged the feelings of joy and misery, of failure and success. As this book was compiled, it felt a data dump of my hard drive, opening space for new information, increasing processing efficiency, or cleaning my garage, purging and sweeping up untidy corners. The reflective trip also confirmed the strong core of beliefs that drove my actions and decisions. Beliefs that were tested, those that evolved, and the unwanted limiting beliefs. Those that were useless, unconsciously adopted, and misaligned were discarded.

I made the effort for deep reflection and self-exploration. When did I bend to the forceful pressure of assimilation? What degree of capitulation was demanded and resisted? How well did I stand firm to my values and beliefs? What was the result of each of these? Did I encourage and promote this for others?

Leadership is most often referenced in singular context, "The Leader." While a leader can forge a new path for others to follow, Believership provides the opportunity for all to lead from within, laying down the foundation, 'paving the road' for all others to travel. It is more permanent and sustainable.

We all have the ability, and many the desire, to lead others along the paved road. In a Believership culture, this multiplies and continues to spread as people are added and the company grows. A single leader-dependent model actually diminishes in value as the employee base and company grow. The leader cannot spread that thin.

Focusing on the power of a single individual creates a limiting environment. The person at the top of an org is not always the best leader, they are the best person to handle the responsibilities of that position - that role, but are they equipped to be a leader?

Many demonstrate exceptional management acumen, wielding influence and commanding performance, but they cannot create Believership. They do not inspire growth in others, or foster belonging, open mindedness, expansion and inclusion. They perpetuate the detrimental patterns that have caused this current state of crisis, steadfast in value extraction rather than value creation and process over people.

We Miss The Obvious And Misinform The Future.

Shawn Achor walks us through a phenomenon called the Tetris Effect in his book, "The Happiness Advantage." Referencing a Harvard Medical School's Department of Psychiatry study, where researches paid 27 students to play Tetris for extended periods over many days. They discovered powerful side effect. (Tetris is a digital game where 4 different shapes from the top of a screen, manipulated by the player to form a solid row at the bottom and rack up as many unbroken lines as possible to gain a score)

What the research discovered was the constant focus on twisting and moving shapes into completed rows, orchestrating this continuous pattern in pursuit of mastery, actually reconfigured the brain, and left the subjects dreaming about the shapes and patterns for days, forming these patterns in everything, seeing them everywhere they went, in every function of their day. Achor writes, "they couldn't stop seeing their world as being made up of sequences of Tetris blocks" From mentally rearranging bricks in a wall to looking out the widow and imaginatively twisting and turning buildings to sequentially fit together in a completed whole.

This weird after-effect is further explained as "cognitive afterimage," similar to the experience when briefly looking at the sun, then seeing the bright circle blurring your vision for a period of time. Playing Tetris extensively for just a few days actually changed the wiring in their brains.

We experience these types of patterns throughout out daily experiences. People who are stuck in a negative mindset; the complainer, the victim, the vocab-corrector, the "that-won't-work" crew and the "best-practice" proclaimers. They are stuck in a pattern, in cognitive-afterimage, likely are unaware, and therefore can't break out of it.

In the same way, we've created mental models of leadership, reinforced through volumes of messaging and matter-of-fact statements and stories passed along as legend through decades, even centuries. It's becomes what we see. We accept it as truth. This causes us to miss the obvious and subconsciously apply it in perpetuity, as if it were a law of nature, rather than a programmed pattern. By not questioning it, we misinform the future.

We Want A Formula

The leaders of companies, and those we admire from afar or through historic examples, are more different than the same, yet we create and idyllic model.

The best leaders lead many, who then lead many more. They appreciate that they are benefactors of great effort, belief and growth in others. They value contribution, ingenuity, diversity, and embrace the power in their uniqueness and that of others, with varied backgrounds, experiences and perceptions.

We are bombarded with retrospective 'trait & character' comparisons trying to find the magic formula - the common kernel of great leaders. Silliness like, 'the 4 traits Sheryl Sandberg, Jeff Bezos, Steve Jobs have in common.' Or, 'How Warren Buffet, Oprah Winfield, Bill Gates and Sara Blakely lead meetings;' the '7 common characteristics of the world's top CEOs.' As if we can just grab these ingredients, toss them into a blender and consume the magic potion.

They sleep, they eat, they likely brush their teeth and certainly work hard, but there is not a secret code of commonality or a hidden strand of DNA. Contrarily, they are all independently divergent. Not the norm. Not following a pattern. Uncommon. Whatever short list of Superpowers we attempt to assign, there is one absolute shared truth: A lot of people contributed alongside of them with hard work, following because they believed in the person, the product, mission or vision. These leaders led people. People made the decision to attach their belief, their goals and ambitions to the leader and or the cause. And they committed. Many will even commit, despite the personality and behaviors of the leader. Each leader is unique, which attracts other unique individuals, allowing them to align and perform. This choice, this commitment from others, is the real superpower of leadership. They inspired Believership.

Weber, Taylor and Drucker led us to believe that a rigid set of repeatable rules and dependencies, and consistent, orchestrated patterns were the backbone and nervous system of organizational excellence. In hindsight, we can recount as many failures as successes, and flaws as proofs points. It's theory that fell apart in practice because it does not consider the great variable - Humans. The theories largely consider humans as common, interchangeable tools, adhering to a model explicitly built on the premise that everyone below the other in the org structure, the value chain, is less-than the one above.

The value chain has shifted. The belief and structure have been slow to respond. The barrier is our quixotic view on leadership.

The Leadership Rub

The responsibilities and pressures on the CEO and ELT of a public traded corporation are different than a private company. Changing the corporate culture and the leadership philosophy is riskier because of the extended influences and stakeholders. Yet, often times it is the leader of the larger corporations that has the visionary beliefs to make bold adjustments. They recognize the significant dependency on other leaders throughout the organization. Establishing a model for leadership is critical and must be intentional.

Smaller, private companies are built on the personality and preferences of the executive, often the person who started the company. The development and advancement of the leadership philosophy is highly dependent on that one person, centered in their personal belief, and often inflexible.

As we gain experience and knowledge, we develop a greater context to learn, which allows deeper learning. Assessing what new ideas and influences to contemplate and consider, has matured. The discipline is to exercise and maintain an open mind. Age does not determine this growth – you don't have to be smart to grow old.

The paradox is that as people develop experiences and age, they often become more rigid in their thinking rather than more discerning and open. These people cannot innovate. They will resist change.

To understand the past, it needs to be viewed through varied perspectives. As a leader, unchecked beliefs and a rigid mind are a detriment to the development of your teams, the growth of your company and likely holding you in harm's way in this rapidly changing business climate.

We've Been Looking Through
A Microscope Not A Telescope

Believership has always been present. Much has been written on this leadership phenomenon throughout time, yet it has continuously been pushed aside, hidden from site, as the 'great-man' theory of stoic heroism commanded the spotlight. The process of selection and ascension is desperately broken, yet met with a mere shrug. We've focused our attention on how to prove a broken model to be true, analyzing historic leadership figures and history through a microscope.

We cling to examples of great business acumen, any authority figure with power to affect others, and mistake it for leadership. An extraordinary example of knowledge, decision-making, influence and business acumen was displayed in Jack Welsh as he turned around GE. Legendary display of management know-how and savvy, he certainly was a leader, yet the implementation and reliance on stack-ranking commanded his power through fear. People were forced to adhere to leadership for fear of being fired - economic insecurity in a troubled time. That one lever was the primary management philosophy. Comply or die. This is still prevalent in many organizations, although GE, Microsoft (after Balmer), Google and many others have since abandoned the uninspiring, dehumanizing ethos.

Seriously think through the repression of stack-ranking – throwing everyone into a bucket and forcing them to climb over each other to get to the surface, leaving a layer of carnage at the bottom that gets washed out. This carnage at the bottom of the bucket is likely to include a lot of good people that helped others, not just themselves, and in turn sacrificed themselves for the benefit of others – the very character of people we would want in a healthy, prosperous environment. People that clutch power can command short bursts of energy, create short-term results, but cannot back it up with strength and longevity.

Believership demonstrates an endless well of continuous surges and consistent renewal of strength. It allows for natural rhythms of innovation, adaptation and sustainable growth. It allows the best to rise, identify and model the behaviors for others, promotes constant maturity and creates an environment where individuals, groups and the business can flourish.

I Didn't Take The Advice

There I stood in Cabo at the President's club award trip having over-performed with my team against the annual targets, trophy in hand, bonus in the bank, and I'm pulled aside by the consulting commander for the CEO. He explained that my performance was certainly exceptional, but they didn't like the way I led. I was too close to my team and unconventional in my approach. The criticisms were, "your team loves you, but," and "it's odd that everyone is comfortable enough to huge when they see each other." Repulsive as it appeared to them, I thought it was a good thing. In a belittling mannor, it was made clear that I didn't fit with their model of executive leadership, and I needed to change - to be more like them. After 3 years with the company, navigating through extraordinary transformation and turmoil, I left Cabo knowing that I was leaving the company. I did not aspire to be like them.

Today, I work companies, teams and leaders, attend seminars, read and listen to 'experts,' that basically pontificate on the existing state of business and leadership, beholden to and fixated on these broken models. It's like they're still trying to figure out how business works. There are always nuances and complexity, but we know how business works. We know all the various organizational models. We have operations, processes, methods, assessments, governance and control structures, and measures all covered. It's seriously more than you can consume - like an endless buffet of options, and all you can eat. While these are necessary to manage process, they are more often barriers to innovation and limitations to human capacity.

Mastery of fundamental business skills, critically important to understand to make good decisions, has little to do with leadership, is void of understanding culture, and completely misses the extraordinary power of Believership. While it may suffice as strong management, it is not leadership, not focused on humans.

I learned more about how to lead by watching other's blunder - from what not to do, than through any guidance on what to do. I resisted the frequent commands to change who I am, to become who they told me to be if I wanted to "fit" in the inner circle of the executive leadership team and continue to advance. I have witnessed bad behaviors and egocentric drivers to the point of absurdity.

I found myself shaking my head at the ineffectively righteous business operations, and joyfully remembering the people I shared the experiences with. And great value was gained with the hindsight vision of experiences, decisions and beliefs - mine and others.

Believership was always there, it's what others experienced, it was the quiet engine - it was unseen. We tend to get down on the things we are not up on. We quickly dismiss what we don't see, and adhere to the comfort of our own lens - our point of view - what we know, rather than what we can envision. Get out of the microscope and flip it to a telescope.

We've been programmed to believe that leaders separate from and stand out. Leadership is within, throughout and all around us - within yourself, within your group and sphere of influence. Leaders are amongst us every day, yet we miss it because we are looking at a false, prototypical model. It's not the authority, it's not the servant, it's not someone else. Leadership is the one who acts with belief; naturally, confidently and consistently. They are not a prescribed container of odd or supernatural traits, characteristics, knowledge or behaviors — it's those that proceed whether accepted or not, living true to who they are. They believe. Others come to believe. They all advance.

A critical difference in those that succeed is they accept and own the responsibility. They own their decisions. They are accountable, knowing they can't pass on responsibility, but they can share authority. Believership is more of an awakening to what has really been going on forever. Through the lens of our current operating systems and unchecked, programmed beliefs, we've misplaced reality with mythical models and then built the case around them with resolute justification.

Understanding and exploring Believership is a move to evolution rather than a revolution. We get caught in the negative battle - the conflict and emotion of fight and conquer as a purpose. We fight to be right, rather than commit to becoming better.

Believership allows us to move together and accelerate positive change. It allows inclusiveness, finds its strength in peace and empowerment. It's expanded through genuineness and kindness. We can usher in the adoption of change piece by piece, with clearer choice and desire for better - desire for change. Following the ineffective trends loudly clanging in our ears today, accepting the cognitive afterimage of unchallenged myths - we'll miss it.

Chapter 4:

The Journey Ahead

"Opportunity comes to pass—not to pause," said James Wallace.

Centuries ago fishermen, explorers and conquerors alike had to become masters at reading the tide, waiting and watching for the precise timing to make it ashore. They faced great risk of either crashing into the rocky harbor or drifting and waiting for the next tide cycle; in Latin, this is known as 'Ob Portu.'

Shakespeare applies this sea-savvy wisdom in his play, 'Julius Caesar,' as Brutus speaks:

> "There is a tide in the affairs of men,
> Which, taken at the flood, leads on to fortune;
> Omitted, all the voyage of their life
> Is bound in shallows and in miseries.
> On such a full sea are we now afloat;
> And we must take the current when it serves,
> Or lose our venture."

Forty years ago, when Robert Geenleaf shared his servant story, seems like a long time, right? And around 1599 when Shakespeare penned this play, certainly was very long ago. Shakespeare was reflecting on the life of one of most prolific "leaders" of all time, in ancient 44 BC, when conspired on and murdered by his close court of Roman senators in the Theatre of Pompey. A very, very long time ago. Indeed, there comes a time. I believe that time is now.

By Force or Choice, Things Change.

We either choose to create change, or change happens to us. Servant Leadership was offered up in 1977, and 42 years later we remain adrift at sea, unable to master 'Ob Portu.' The opportunity has been there. Attempts have been made, but the tide of the industrial mindset has persisted, and the progression of these enlightened ideals remain nascent. Partly due to the benign implementation that attempted to fold this transformative ideal comfortably into the existing structures - trying to bring the ship to harbor without rocking the boat - and largely because there was not a compelling need to change.

That compelling, critical time is upon us. We stand at a clearly researched, documented and widely accepted gap. Capacity of our workforce is low and the demands, the need, is unprecedentedly high. People are fed up, burnt out and largely disengaged, while change is swirling at us with increasing velocity, an upheaval in business we've not experienced before.

The slow response to this obvious challenge is troubling yet expected. The Julius Caesar's of our day, the archetypes we continue to select and place in leadership, have little incentive to shake the status quo. This is also changing. With trillions of capital value at stake each year, and clear forecast it will escalate, the current path is not sustainable - the need for sweeping change is undeniable. The question now becomes, how - and how fast - can we make it happen?

Awareness exists. Prescriptive programs and implementation opportunities exists in large scale. Recognition of the urgent need exists. Yet we adopt change in slow motion.

Why the resistance? We have the wrong leaders in place and are mesmerized by the promise of process automation and methodology. We are beholden to the belief that the end-state must be clear (latent-perfectionism), and we keep waiting for the solution to come from the same source that is part of the problem, or as Einstein shared, "We cannot solve our problems with the same thinking we used when we created them." In this case, depending on institutions, governments, universities, major consultancies to drive us forward at the required pace. These institutions are in desperate need of the solution - they cannot create it.

We Saw It Coming

Each individual develops their beliefs and bring them wherever they go, building on it, and attaching it to the organization; the one they are in or the one they are moving to. No longer does the corporation, the brand of the entity have greater value than the brand of the employee. This is a major shift in the past 10 years. Although we could imagine the possibilities of change, the reality outpaced the predictions, and the scale of disruption has been and continues to be huge.

In 2008 Clay Shirky wrote the book, "Here Comes Everyone." Throughout, he explores the major shifts underway with bandwidth expansion, smartphones, and apps, to quickly created networks of immediate communication around the world. He talks about how it enhanced our ability to solve social problems, the amazement of Wikipedia, personal media/branding and other seemingly interesting examples of the time. It's almost laughable now, as Uber, Airbnb, Instagram weren't invented, Twitter and YouTube were fledgling toddlers, but Shirky did hit on a profound reality: "Collective action, where a group acts as a whole, is even more complex than collaborative production, but here again new tools give life to new forms of action. This in turn challenges exiting institutions, by eroding the institutional monopoly on large-scale coordination." This new reality was largely ignored - we now know better.

Imagine the era I grew up in. You're recruited out of college and the information you're taught, the authority/leadership you're exposed to is the only model presented. You are forced to emulate these beliefs and behaviors, and shelter yourself into the ignorance of options and alternatives, rewarding those that 'fit in' to advance. Today, people early in their career can be sitting in a company townhall meeting listening to the CEO, perhaps shaking their heads in disagreement, and pulling up a dozen YouTube videos and podcasts of leaders with a different point of view, a better idea or approach, that aligns with their beliefs. Blindly following authority is gone forever. People need to believe, and they have choices.

Just like each employee now brings their own technology, networks and experiences to the job - they also bring their own brand. This has evolved rapidly in past few years with unlimited content to consume and share, and the plethora of choices we have on where to gather information. It's not a completely new phenomenon. Salespeople have been wooed into companies because they have valuable client relationships that will continue on with the individual, carried from company to company. We must embrace the paradigm shift that the primary value is now the relationships, the people, not the entity.

These institutional shifts are in clear and compelling view. We will continue to progress toward self-belief and personal choice. There will be a demand for personal growth, not the age-old career-track nonsense that dictates learning programs. We will value alignment over assimilation — Voice over silence and Listening over commanding. No longer will value be assessed from the outside or progression to our goals be set within the rigor of institutional hierarchy. Self-Belief and alignment will be the driver to decide if the top talent wants to attach their brand to a leader - not a command of obligation or duty. Disappearing are the one-sided contracts and commitments to hold someone hostage. People will liberate themselves from this system. A system that operates with the fundamental premise that the paycheck has a greater value than the Human Spirit. These days are ending.

It's Not What We've Done, It's What We Do Next

In a May, 2019 Foundation for Economic Education article from Mark J. Perry, *a scholar at the American Enterprise Institute, comparing the Fortune 500 from 1955-2019, writes (paraphrased);*

Comparing the 1955 *to* 2019 *Fortune 500*, only 10.4 percent (52 companies) have remained on the list, and more than 89 percent of the companies from 1955 have either gone bankrupt, merged, shrunk and fallen from the list. There's been a lot of market disruption, churning, and Schumpeterian creative destruction over the last six decades. And change is accelerating, disruption opportunities are significant with technological advances and the lack of ability to adapt to the dynamism and innovation that characterizes a vibrant consumer-oriented market economy, in today's hyper-competitive global economy.

Corporations in the S&P 500 Index in 1965 stayed in the index for an average of 33 years. By 1990, it narrowed to 20 years, and forecast to shrink to 14 years by 2026. About half of today's S&P 500 firms will be replaced over the next 10 years as in this period of heightened volatility, shaping up to be the most potentially turbulent in modern history" according to [various research].

There are many different factors that contribute to these changes, affecting nearly all industries. The general response is to double down on current operational patterns, programs, structures and leadership beliefs. And the rate of failure, with a very high price tag, continues to climb.

We need to stop staring at the problem.

We're blinded by what's right in front of us, and when we're looking at it in with a fresh, future-looking perspective, we can see what the possible solutions will be. Resisting, and continuing to do the same things hoping it will get better, is insane. Some refuse to acknowledge the shift has already occurred, and hold fast to the past. It gives them some sense of plausible denial, circumstances beyond their control, an excuse for not taking the responsibility to solve the problem.

Find a solution, decide to fix the problem. How do we go about that? We look at the human elements, our capacity and self-imposed limitations dig deep on what's really going on in our value and belief systems.

We Can Do Better

Believership is a superpower beyond leadership because it resides within each one of us. It is not dependent on what we are told, nor is it beholden to a figurehead or an individual in charge. It's not dependent on the 'great-person' fable forced onto us as an institutional default that doesn't hold up under scrutiny in view of enhanced perspectives and current-day challenges.

Accumulation of many experiences and observations of others; what I saw work, what I experienced that doesn't work; what I believed and what was in line with those beliefs and my values. The determining factor in speed, attainment of goals, success or failure was how people are treated and treat others. Relationships.

Too often, leadership was taught and described as a singular, rigid belief, like a military regimen where everyone needed to be equal, the same, and measured on a ubiquitous standard. That was absolutely foreign to me and diametrically opposed to the way I experienced the world. I didn't buy it.

I have a strong disdain for bad behavior – prescriptive-authority and commanding behavior. My rejection is more of a disbelief in the concept of sameness, uniformity or normal. I still don't understand what normal means. Normal, to me, is the most abnormal belief.

Winters hit hard in Minnesota. It's cold, windy and snowy. That's normal from November to April. It's not always cold, windy and snowy through those months. I've played golf in January, shoveled 20 inches of snow in May, and been outside enjoying a walk around the lakes on beautiful 80-degree day in March. Those occurrences are abnormal. Over an extended period of time, say a decade, no winter will be the same. Amount of snow, when it starts and stops, length of a sub-zero streak, all vary year to year. Winter is normal – there is no normal winter.

Human beings and relationships are significantly more complex than winter weather patterns. Yet it is common and constant to hear leaders and experts talk about normal behavior, normal situations, normal expectations. It's like a default to an unknown and indescribable state; Nowhere, nothing, everywhere, everything. Without clarity and definition, it's meaningless.

Chapter 5:

Impact And Scale

To fully understand and embrace the shift to Believership, we must answer the question: What happens because of you?"

Exploring your impact as a leader, requires a completely new perspective, humility and honesty. This is the path to genuineness. The Give-Get equation has to be wiped clean and re-imagined: Defeat is in the limitation of expectations, the adherence to historic beliefs and patters, understanding that orchestrated outcomes are far less empowered outcomes. While orchestration may be predictable it is restricted. Empowered outcomes are limitless.

Out Of The Head And Into The Soul

Over the past three years, facilitating high-achieving team workshops, consulting on leadership and culture transformation, acquisitions and reorgs, advising CEO's &ELTs, and diligently engaging in conversational research around the world, I uncovered a disturbing truth: that people are taught *not* to find their belief.

Instead they are commanded to believe what they are told. Told to embrace what is forced on them. Told what experience they are supposed to be having, rather than understand and express the experience they are actually having. Told how to behave and what to feel, and often told not to feel at all - just do your job and leave all that baggage at the door.

It's true for the CEO reporting to the board and executive team supporting them. It was enforced at an ever-increasing degree as I worked throughout layers within companies. Our current hierarchal systems press pressure down, subduing creativity, innovation and growth, rather than pulling the ambition, responsibility and capacity upward, fostering discovery, expression and development of belief. When the energy flows up and through an organization, people feel empowered, feel they belong and contribute fully with their heads up and eyes forward.

The key words: People. Feel.

People will not perform at their highest level and seek growth without self-belief. The vast majority of our operational obsession is on measurement. We don't measure people on their growth and capacity, their alignment and progression to personal development goals, we are firmly stuck in measuring them against each other or a bygone standard of output.

We kill hope with the insistent, narrow minded performance management rigor, and ineffective, unimaginative learning and development programs. We never ask the employee how they can align their personal big-picture with the company big-picture, exploring and expanding their beliefs, therefore settle for less in personal attainment and company performance. Our employee experience programs are steeped in the bygone notion of 'hire to retire.' Focused on career path rather than personal development, role fulfillment rather than capacity growth. The company and the individual are short-changed.

The mindset shift is to allow this evolution from contraction to expansion. Attracting and hiring the best talent then forming them into existing corporate molds to fulfill commands and expectations (expressed and unexpressed), shuts down possibilities, stifling innovation and contribution. To grow capacity and meet the demands of current and future state, we need to emancipate people, corporate cultures, and our belief system from the rigid structures of measurement and assimilation.

Freedom To Choose

In a nearly ubiquitously connected world, with growing opportunity for remote and distributed work, and new models, new companies, emerging in disruptive succession, people have more choice than ever before, and choice is freedom.

Retention is no longer a 'hostage' situation, contrived and controlled by authority and threat, buy carrot and stick, it becomes personal choice and that choice is based on belief in vision mission, of the company and the leader. When people believe they can continue to grow personally and their contribution is acknowledged and valued they will be compelled to stay, to keep growing, gaining capacity and keep contributing at a high level. When this doesn't exist, they already have a foot out the door, with a watchful eye on new opportunities.

The more companies try to control, the less control they have.

Milton Hershey was an innovative and good-hearted man. His relentless pursuit of the best chocolate recipe to launch his Utopian plans for a factory and village is legendary.

Three years after selling his first successful confectionery endeavor, Lancaster Caramel Company, he began building a world-class facility in Derry Church. As the company grew and Hershey's wealth expanded, so did his vision for creating a model community. In the town that came to be known as Hershey, Pennsylvania, Hershey built schools, churches, museums, parks, stadiums and housing and even a trolley system for his workers.

His philanthropy was cause based, and big hearted. Hershey was committed to the well-being of his workforce, his villagers, as a workers and citizens. He even kept his employees during the recession, but trouble still came. It was a growth cycle for unions, and as profits soared, the investment in the community at large was less appreciated and people wanted personal reward, personal growth at their discretion, rather than through another's perception of need. People lost belief in their leader. They revolted with a work-stopping and supply chain killing strike. Chaos erupted and was never the same. All were left unfulfilled.

People need to believe. Without Believership, leadership is merely a position - a role. Without the opportunity and encouragement for people grow their self-belief, exercise and align their values, needs, and ambitions, employment will remain a transaction - time and effort in exchange for money. The value of the contribution will always be a back and forth struggle, and the authoritarian leadership model will remain in place.

To generate the energy needed to leap forward and address the widening gap between the current state of human capacity and the accelerating wave of disruption, self-leadership is a necessity. In a corporate environment, self-leadership is better described as guided governance." This is a critical, yet rare, skill for future leaders, as it is not taught. In complex organizations, this approach empowers with intent rather than control. Implemented well, accountability shifts to the individual and their peers, which enables expansion of capacity and continuity.

One iconic leader cannot command a company, a village, a distributed workforce as days of old. When we open the opportunity for all to seek their mission, grow along the path of their desire, encouraged to explore and expand, the best will rise. We will attract, develop and open our minds to varied experiences, backgrounds, expanded values and honor personal choice. We will have the diversity we know is needed, because we allowed it, not orchestrated or forced it. With this inclusivity, outdated models of selection can be retired.

Putting Believership Into Action

We've outgrown the extant 4-word leadership strategy, "because I said so." It's one thing to inspire commitment through command or a sense of duty and very different, evolved state to experience commitment from belief, a heart-centered feeling of purpose and desire - putting love into action.

This is beautifully captured in the book, "Evolved Executive: The Future of Work is Love in Action" by my friend and HumansFirst collaborator, Heather Hanson Wickman.

Her research is deep, establishing a powerful case for making a radical and rapid shift to triage the crisis of suffering we've created with abhorrent leadership practices, and boost us on to the path of organizational health. It starts with examining and changing our limiting beliefs, replacing the fear-based standard with a higher consciousness and then circle back to adjust our structures and team practices.

She asks, "When was the last time you paid attention to the health and dynamics of your living, breathing system you call your company? Your employees do the work, but what do you really know about them? When was the last time you checked in on their lives? Do you know what obstacles are in their way? Do you know what gives them a sense of meaning and purpose? Have you asked them for feedback on how you could better support their work?"

If you're a leader and can't easily answer these questions, you're not leading, you're managing or commanding, and your people don't believe in you. How can they?

Until we change our hearts, we cannot change our minds. We must change our minds to survive and grow in this very different, non-industrial era.

Change is accelerating. Bridge builders used to be the program managers and process orchestrators. Now they are the change makers. Solution seekers, leaders, need to be comfortable with chaos to keep the bridge builders focused, engaged, energize and constantly learning.

A few key tenets need to be in place. Vulnerability - not as frightening as you think. Vulnerability for leaders isn't a radical shift in personality. It can be a simple small step in the right direction, and built on from there, piece by piece. A very simple, yet powerful behavior tweak is adopting the willingness to change your mind. Vulnerability is a strength in leadership. If you're not aware enough to know and own your limitations, the flaw in a past decisions or manor of conducting business - that's weakness. If you are not on a growth path, expanding your awareness, beliefs and limitations, you have a huge blind spot.

If you have responsibility for others without the capacity to shoulder their burden, requiring empathy, you're not a leader. If these are not yet core to your culture, start here. So much is written, and the benefits are clear to have empathy at the center of your values and visible in your behaviors. The oft-quoted, "culture eats strategy" and the high degree of focus on the benefits of healthy culture (the everyday experience in and with your company), speaks to the up-side. Of greater concern is down-side of a bad culture. If you don't believe prioritizing cultural improvement as a value enhancer - be painfully aware of the damage a poor culture can have on your business.

Action starts with you. Then your team, and then throughout the company. Don't wait for permission, don't wait for leadership. Don't wait to be told. Act. It's your experience, your hope and belief. It's about relationships, passion, connection and belonging. Importantly, it is about growing and sustaining a culture of value creation rather than extraction. Hilton Barbour captures this compelling wisdom in his blog full of gems, " the biggest issue is how to gain emotional commitment, which translates to managers taking on company success as a personal crusade and so is worth more than financial, intellectual and physical commitment combined."

In a personal exchange with Jeffrey Pfeffer, author of "Dying For A Paycheck," I asked what outcomes he would be interested in learning as we went around the country having open-interactive discussions with hundreds of people at the HumansFirst events? His strong interest and encouragement were to build a case to take to OSHA, as the level of harm done in toxic, poorly led companies had reached an epidemic level and progress toward improvement was slow - as if no one was really paying attention. I thanked him, yet assured him I had no appetite for approaching a government agency. My belief is in people above institutions. In our ability to change, rather than calling on and waiting for someone else.

Consider the epidemic he was pointing to in the conversation, which is called out in his Stanford research and shared in his book, 120,000 unnecessary deaths are caused each year by workplace stress, toxic emotional environments and bad bosses. This is the 5th on the leading cause of death in the United States. Comparatively, nearly 34,000 lost their lives to gun violence, rightfully capturing our attention, and less than 150 fatalities per year on the OSHA regulated construction industry. (120,000 | 34,000 | 150).

Change And Discomfort

Love is the only force powerful enough to play in the sandbox with fear and greed. Love is a gift, rather than a tool or weapon. Being a gift bearer will feel uncomfortable. Bring gifts anyway. Become comfortable with the discomfort. Change is necessary.

We have to encourage individual thinking, honoring what is important to each person. We learn differently, we're motivated differently, and we have to be empowered to create our own paths. We also have to be aligned. Knowing what our objectives are and how we get there is really important. How we interact in team communications. How we run our meetings. Flexing and adapting the rhythms and the agenda to keep up with the flow of change. What comes out of that is better focus, greater energy, flexibility for quicker outcomes, and perhaps better meetings. Everybody understands their contribution their role and connection to others. The critical next piece is maturity and a better understanding how we interact with each other. And that's what a team is, that is what culture is, that is what a company is, that is what business is. We're humans. We have to be fulfilled and satisfied through that journey.

The great business of the future will have made the decision to stop proving and start improving. They will painfully recognize that simply doing more of the same, putting all their energy and resources trying to make the same, better - Is not better - it's more of the same.

Purpose is another huge field of debate and exploration. It is important to address and have clearly articulated understanding for yourself and everyone in your organization. Allow for multiple views and personalization, this will not be a uniform belief.

Allowing people to explore, understand and then align their purpose with the company for the part of the journey you share, them as an employee, you as a company, and between one another as colleagues, is the enlightened rarely experienced approach.

Personally, I believe it is discovered along the path. It's not a catalog of options, available in profile quiz or drop-down list. We must be in motion and open to purpose. It's not seek and find, it's progress toward, and it's not a destination, it is the journey. Purpose is developed and discovered from within, when we are aware of beliefs. Live with a belief-core and seek growth, movement, learning. Exercise openness and awareness. From the developing beliefs and maturation of how we interact with the world, purpose rises from our heart.

We Learn, We Grow, We Change

Want to be a part of a great company? Become great. You want to build a great company? Focus on developing people. People produce the value of your business. People create and produce product and services. People lead. People operate and manage. People sell. People are your culture. People are your customers. Your business is based on humans. Put HumansFirst.

We have a lot of work do. First of all, break patterns. Move away from the expected, that which was handed down, and create the experience you envision. Like the circles of Zorro, start small where you can master it, then within your close associates, and keep progressing. Know the patterns, dissect the fault and understand the unique beliefs and needs of others. Importantly, diligently assess, reflect and adjust biased beliefs that have "naturally" developed or have been adopted but are misaligned. Assimilation is sneaky, slowly chipping away at your beliefs, values and ambitions.

Take on more so you can give more back. Stop contemplating and start achieving, people depend on you whether it's acknowledged or not. Be a great teammate. There is not an invite or coronation. It's not a social event, not a frat or sorority, not a family gathering. Show up as yourself every day, pay some dues, understand timing with patient awareness and always believe you belong. You belong through contribution, through support of others and comprehension of the whole. Turn the scoreboard on, set goals, keep score, run the clock. This is your life, so play, learn and keep growing.

The greatest choice we have each day is our attitude. John Maxwell wrote two great books on the topic, "Today Matters," and "The Difference Maker." They're old books, probably pennies at a used bookstore. They'll remind you that you have choice, and choice is a great freedom.

Positivity requires an understanding that everyone has their own journey that we know little about - we all have "stuff." Own yours, stop complaining and you'll be on your way to greater happiness. We have too many excuses, to many options for blaming others. Blame and excuses are rooted in fear and doubt. Ask more questions, challenge yourself to have a beginner's mindset, be curious and get over yourself (move ego aside). Understand that there is no such thing as a level playing field and nothing is equal. So, stop comparing, embrace the freedom of not being the same, equal or level. Be the best you, better each day.

Sounds like advice to a first-year professional doesn't it? It certainly applies for them, but this is advice to CEO's and the many corporate executives I've engaged with through my career. These were, are for some, the missing elements of your company's, your employee's success. Positivity is your responsibility first. You're a leader - or you're not. People believe – or they don't.

This is essential to creating Believership cultures for exponential and sustainable growth with the agility to adapt and change to the shifting landscape.

We can help each other through these barriers, and it is critically important that a support network and safe environment and relationships are available to talk it through, keep moving and get past the barriers. To reach our potential and continuously expand our capacity, it is imperative that we connect, listen, understand and help.

In The Complexity Of Doing, We Lose Perspective

HR has a role in this, but the business has the responsibility to train and prepare young people - their world is changing, fast and constant, and there is no way for a systemic, process-driven approach to address personal development.

We're failing miserably at this. Within the first 3 years of professional work, most employees are questioning everything about the experience. I was fortunate. Was not tossed on the potter-wheel, carved and molded into someone else's interpretation of who I needed to be and how I need to think and act. I was a "free-roaming" adult for 20 years. But I've seen my children and their friends, and the hundreds of young people I've coached and thousands that worked on my teams go through, or share with me, their experience.

The answers to transformation success for leadership and HR are in the future, not in the past. We haven't been faced with the multi-faceted challenges presented today, therefore we must envision the future to create the solutions. Take a shot at significance. Status quo leads to dissatisfaction, disengagement, and is crippling to business growth.

Consistency over perfection is a motto (and t-shirt) my son shares with his strength and nutrition clients. It also stands as a perfect motto for organizational development. Understanding the potential gains from technology advancement, AI, digital transformation is critical to advance our organizations and enhance our human capacity. Yet our imagination has stalled, reverting back to what we know and driving decision makers to retro fit old processes rather than envision new solutions. Operational departments, and executive teams continue to make decisions with a "procurement as strategy" belief, focusing on the features and functions, the marketing hype, with a belief that positive change can simply be purchased. The next big universal fix is unlikely to create positive change. If it was available, every business would have already deployed it. The value is in adoption. Adoption success is based on people. Until we envision and create human value, the failure rate will continue to escalate.

Pick a priority, do it well and consistently, and transform first into an iterative rhythm of change. Start with purging the unnecessary processes, explore and adjust the laggard, limiting beliefs in models that have not, will not work. Consistent small changes over time create big shifts. We don't fully know what is going to work, what is needed until we get close enough to gain perspective and reach the right 'altitude' to make decisions. Engage excessively in communication. This is the great change.

It won't be perfect. Humans make mistakes. We cannot expect perfection from others, nor ourselves. Tech won't solve it. People are the solution – it is not easy. Allow mishaps – learn, help, support. You're in business, which means to address change at the speed of business, you have to drop the academic mindset - "empirical" is theory and proof is a lagging indicator of truth. Truth in business is experienced through people, not statistics and process. Don't confuse results for truth. It's feelings and outcomes that create belief and motivate action. Can you prove a 'best practice' outcome, or a feeling? No. You can foster, understand, channel and measure the belief of people. Get this right, and accelerated, consistent adoption of change is possible.

People need choice and open options for learning that align with their personal growth plan - not yours. When they are excitedly in pursuit of their dreams, they will be able to align and fully perform for the business.

These are the 2 greatest failings of HR - and the 2 greatest opportunities for HR. Neither are solved through technology procurement, or academic theory. While there is a lot activity and noise about disruption and transformation within the HR 'industry,' it continues to point in the wrong direction, inwardly focused on the inner workings of the profession, deploying systemic process and ignoring the human part of the 'resource.'

This is the greatest time of need and opportunity for HR. The time is now to re-invent, not re-position.

Great works are being done by visionary leaders in companies, innovative forums, and progressive academic programs. These are leaders who are stepping up and meeting the challenge, they are transforming not conforming, and forging divergent paths forward for others to follow. I'm fortunate to call many of them friends, learning and collaborating.

"What you chose to stop doing is as important as what you choose to do next"

The call to action from expert sources is plentiful, still the propensity to adopt change is steeped in historical justification and denial. A peek at an excerpt from Bersin by Deloitte:

> [Driven by the ongoing digital revolution and demographic, political, and social forces, almost 90 percent of HR and business leaders rate building the organization of the future as their highest priority. In its 2017 Global Human Capital Trends report, Deloitte issues a call-to-action for companies to completely reconsider their organizational structure, talent and HR strategies to keep pace with digital disruption.

> "Technology is advancing at an unprecedented rate and these innovations have completely transformed the way we live, work and communicate," said Josh Bersin. "Ultimately, the digital world of work has changed the rules of business. Organizations should shift their entire mind-set and behaviors to ensure they can lead, organize, motivate, manage and engage the 21st century workforce, or risk being left behind. Deloitte finds that HR is struggling to keep up."

As an organizational body, with extensive ties to industry experts and academics, who've been tracking, reporting and advising HR through decades, and we find ourselves standing in a very bad place, arguably creating a case that they are a part of the problem, not the solution. With extensive data, research, theories, trials and lessons, they have led us to place in history when things are worse and worsening, not better and improving. First rule when you find yourself in a hole is to stop digging. Yet the "HR-Industry" at large and their governing organizations stand firm holding their shovels.

It is you, the committed and dedicated practitioner that is going to initiate the climb out of this deep and dark hole. You know how disruptive business changes are affecting your world, your people, and your company. You are called to act and make decisions each day that impact people and the success of your company. The pontificators will not stand with you. They will not lift you up, they have no horse in the race. Be a problem solver. Work with problem solvers. Be bold. Change fast and drastically.

Cathy Benko and Erica Volini from Deloitte offer more layers of difficulty:

"A recent survey of CEOs reveals that HR is overwhelmingly viewed as the least agile function. In our own conversations with CFOs we consistently hear that their attempts to work strategically with HR are the most trying. Business leaders concur, with nearly 50 percent reporting that HR is not ready to lead. Even HR itself agrees. In a global survey, HR and talent executives graded themselves a C-minus for overall performance, citing a large capability shortfall, with 77 percent of respondents ranking the need to re-skill the HR function among the top quartile of their priorities.

These days, the scarcity impeding firms' growth is not of capital — it's of talent. We live in an era where eight five percent of value creation stems from brand, intellectual property, and people — all intangible assets. Delivering HR-related operational, compliance, and administrative tasks with distinction is important, but let's be clear that doing so is table stakes. The CHRO must step up to the implications of the new world of work."

Business is fluid. We must achieve during transformation, not wait it out and withdraw until it is complete, assessed and assured. To move forward with the required velocity and scale, we need a clear understanding of "transformation."

Transformation is taking something that exists and making something different. You can't say transformation when referring to your continuous improvement program, that's called continuous improvement; taking something that exists and making it better. Transformation happens when you make significant, multifaceted, interrelated changes. You can't get to the desired destination by perpetuating the same programs, behaviors and thinking in the operational state today. Break patterns to set new priorities and purge the old and ineffective – even it is believed to be a HR standardized best practice.

Chapter 6:

Superpowers

Believership is the Superpower beyond leadership because it is the one certain thing that great leaders have in common; people believed. They inspired belief in them, as a leader, their vision or mission. Of the great leaders we have experienced or have read about, it was not a common set of skills, personality traits, or extraordinary acumen that we can profile and replicate in another, it was their uniqueness and ability to inspire the belief of others, gaining their commitment.

A compelling, underlying theme of Superhero movies is the story of redemption. A common experience of Superheroes is isolation due to their uniqueness. We see them struggle, with separation from the represented norm, battling inside and outside forces. We're drawn in to empathize with their emotional conflict, yet become inspired with their resilience, perseverance and resolve.

The fundamental roles we experience in these tales are: Villain, Victim, Bystander, and Superhero. We can readily apply these roles to people we experience everyday in business, from top of an org to the bottom. The CEO that is quick to pin troubles on other's mistakes or blames the market or outside conditions – Victim. The person that complains about their lack of influence and choice to create change because the environment of other people – Victim or Bystander. The managers that perpetuate status quo and surrender the behaviors and pressures as a means of self-protection – Bystander or Villain. Bystanders are generally the majority, waiting for and relying on someone else. The true villains are all around us. They are the demeaning and unfit that create the toxic environments, push pressure down rather than owning responsibility, and cause stress throughout their realm of influence. Like a virus, their broken belief system and negativity spreads rampant, unseen, unchecked.

A recent Harvard study shows that it is almost twice as profitable to eliminate toxic bosses (villains) than to go out and hire top performing ones – villains cost more in profit loss, than superheroes can generate. Why do we tolerate this? What organization norms have we surrendered to? And why do we remain adherent to the flawed archetypical profile that we use to select and promote bad leaders?

We've misplaced the model of leadership, we promote villains and bystanders and often victims, those that have shunned responsibility and sacrificed character, their souls in the climb to the top. More than ever, we need Superheroes.

Leaders with these superpowers rise above the challenge and bring goodness for the value of others. Whether loathed or lauded, redemption comes from their contribution to a greater whole - something far bigger than themselves, served by their unique gifts. They are real, genuine to their uniqueness and accountable to themselves and others.

They are known as courageous, with a strong moral code, mental stability, pain tolerant, responsible, knowledgeable with great instincts, tenacity and perseverance, and trust.

Leaders that create Believership have this in common — they have superpowers that are often overlooked, hidden or even denied, and it is only through contribution to others and a mission greater than themselves, that these powers manifest in glorious fashion to achieve extraordinary results. We need these superheroes now more than ever.

There Is No Normal

Try as you may to weave a common a thread through the admired leaders of modern day, especially in business, there is no normal. It is only through the narrow, foggy lens of organizational norms rooted in the industrial century of the past, that we are ridiculous enough to even ponder this absurdity.

Norms are limitations. Like comfort food for our brains, we subconsciously crave it. While perhaps comforting, we don't need it and it's not our best choice. Greatness is abnormal, at times seemingly reckless. In all cases great leaders fight the constraints force upon them and move forward with resolve. People believe in them or what they are doing, or what they stand for, and the attach themselves, with commitment. It's not a lead and follow situation. It's *with*. When Believership is present, people align with the leader.

Skills Rely on Power But Are Not Powerful

We've accepted a narrow and generic definition of leadership and management based on a common set of skills and traits. There are aptitudes, abilities and characteristics that can be recognized and cultivated, and we must put a critical effort forward to make sure we have assessed accurately that these are the ones we want, not simply the hand-me-down ideals of the past. As we make these assessments and decisions, we need to make a fundamental distinction: management and leadership are separate things, two different sets of skills, necessarily performed in parallel.

Management is a set of skills improved with experience, knowledge and capacity to learn, all the way to the point of mastery, where it becomes nearly an art form. Command of process, organizational awareness, decision making, consistency and the ability to operate from high altitude to ground level, and orchestrate flow through the structural dimensions of complex business and economies can be amazing. I respect great management skills.

Leadership is about people. This is what separates leadership from management; business is managed, people are led. If you believe you can manage people, you've likely not parented a teenager, or coached a youth sports team.

Carlo Collodi (Lorenzini) illustrated this long-known truth in his classic adventures of Pinocchio. A puppet can be managed, it's the orchestration skills of the puppeteer that are in control. But when those strings are cut, were treated with the adventures of a naughty disobedient child who must learn to be good, for himself, others and society, to prove that he is worthy of becoming a real boy. "Cut the strings" on management and leadership is required.

The management/leadership lines are entangled in the hierarchy-beholden world to the past century of Weberism, Taylorism and Druckerism. As any multi-generational belief system, separating from the entanglement is an arduous task. Like untangling a huge ball of holiday lights; finding an end, loosening the knot, weaving the increasingly long loose end back through the knotted core without breaking off the bulbs and damaging the whole string, is near wizardry.

Military leadership models different from business in one key element; the assignment of will. When entering the military, you sign up to the chain of command, surrendering personal will for the greater good of the others and the whole. It's remarkable and honorable, and greatly appreciated. This distinction can make it difficult in transitioning to civilian leadership. Most have the ability and capacity to lead, possessing the aforementioned traits of superheroes. Shifting their mental model from command, which is more management, to willful engagement, which is business leadership, is the mainspring.

Likewise, many of the iconic leaders over the past century were great managers, afforded the environment to command structural adherence. That was the system. That was the norm. An authoritative business manager could wield control, leveraging process over people to drive results. This standard of operation birthed the abhorrently still-practiced top-grading theory of management to the forefront. It's a losing model in this modern, non-industrial era, and is rapidly dying, abandoned by the very companies gave it life.

Unconventional Terms Of Engagement

Uniqueness is the energy of Believership, essential to lead the navigation into our modern era. Innovation is now a requirement, not a luxury of genius. Nilofer Merchant's book, "The Power of Onlyness," brings this to light. Summarized, she shares, "Not Everyone Will, But Anyone Can. Nothing matters more than innovation; that something new that creates value.

It's innovation that has allowed us to build today's smartphones, and will let us build tomorrow's teleportation pods. It's innovation that solves centuries' old problems, and lets us invent the future. It's, of course, what makes money and grows our economy to benefit our lives & society.

Bedrock findings from innovation research is that, unlike invention or scientific discovery, innovation (a) emerges from "left-field" sources, and (b) by *connections* between previously separate elements. And yet, the very way we have constructed our societies and the organizations which populate them surely *strangles* the most fruitful forces of innovation. We are long overdue for an alternative conception."

Successfully navigating the turbulence of today's business climate, and accelerating through positive change, requires actively letting go. Let go of self-sabotage - the historic limiting beliefs, the distressed operating models and flawed leadership archetypes.

We have great examples of rising to the challenge.

Satya Nadella calls out the foundations for his leadership in "Hit Refresh," emphasizing empathy first and a learn-it-all not know-it-all mindset throughout the organization. Coming in on the heels of a boastful manager and a $7 billion debacle, Satya did in fact hit refresh, centered on the cloud, led significant cultural shifts, and in 4 years nearly tripled the stock value and shot revenues to $1 Trillion, restoring the company as a world-class leader of this modern era.

Bob Chapman has become an active voice in the power of Believership. Along with Raj Sisodia, their book, "Everybody Matters" explores Chapman's journey to find the best approach to business and leadership. Calling out traditional approaches that treat employees like cogs in the machine, they explain how caring for employees as if they were family, can not only create unprecedented success but inspire company loyalty and allow all employees to reach their full potential.

Along with care and focus on personal growth, they share a few corporate tenets to foster this culture: Create a charter with employee input; give employees freedom to make their own decisions; motivate with strong adherence to these principles.

Heather Hanson Wickman said in a conversation one day, "personal development is a team sport." It has become one of my favorite quotes. Indeed, to have people believe in leadership and the company mission, develop the superpowers of their own unique potential, and learn to lead with heart, it is a team sport.

Strengths And Weakness As Strength

Ambroise Paul Toussaint Jules Valéry speaks to our faults: "We hope vaguely, but dread precisely."

Human skills are the greatest strength.

A core tenet of the idyllic leadership myth is anything outside of rank, authority and regimen was soft. Know the process, take charge, command performance. Always bark, never listen. Mimicking this was the path to more pay and longer stay. You advanced by surrendering your identity, adopting the ethos and ethics to fit with the environment. It's Darwin's world, survival of the fittest - you can't out run the lion, so outrun the other person.

Not sure if this is the mentality in your company? You likely have heard one of these phrases during your employment: That won't work here; it's not the way we do it; won't happen; it is what it is; just do your job; we don't pay you to think; that's above your paygrade, to which the proper response is, "then pay me more."

There is a lot of talk about authenticity, discovering and acting on our beliefs, not adopted behaviors. Vulnerability makes people squirm. What does it mean and how is it possible?

Acting on your beliefs and values, exercising your talents and uniqueness, is a reasonable explanation of authenticity.

Kimberly Davis, author of "Brave Leadership" helps us understand the importance: "So often we turn our identity over to other people. How they define us becomes more important than how we define ourselves. Their opinions of us - of who we are and who we should be - drown out our internal voices. We lose the ability to own ourselves. But what's the price we pay? If every day we feel as if we must pretend to be someone we're not, how does that impact our ability to show up powerfully in this world? I think one of the most important things we can do is honor the person we truly know ourselves to be. For how can we fully show up and bring our gifts and make an impact if we are diminishing our power by disowning our truth? We can't."

Vulnerability for leaders isn't a radical shift in personality. It can be a simple small step in the right direction, and built on from there, piece by piece. A very simple, yet powerful behavior tweak is adopting the willingness to change your mind.

Vulnerability is a strength in leadership: If you're not aware enough to know and own your limitations - that's weakness, and a huge blind spot. If you have responsibility for others without the capacity to shoulder their burden, requiring empathy, you're not a leader. Growing, giving, connecting, maturing – these are vulnerable behaviors. They are necessary and brave and essential for Believership.

Resilience is a science, biological and physical. It is also a key psychological factor, one that can be bolstered and relied on. Having resiliency is core to strong self-belief, the ability to stay the course and bounce back when needed. It's mental toughness and strength, sometimes seen as weakness because you have to stall, struggle or fall to build it. That seems like vulnerability, but is actually required strength. We all experience it, the strong embrace it. They become more resilient, and they are able to consistently persevere.

Choice, Commitment, Change

Perseverance is a strength within us all, and sometimes we forget. Think back to that point in time in your life where you experienced a pivot point, a major change. Go back there, feel that strength and keep it with you. You have the power and freedom of choice. Over the years I've collected so many scars I am never sure which one to pick when opening up and truly exploring my belief in embracing big change, in believing the outcome without seeing it - persevering. This one stays with me:

I'd always wanted to be a pro athlete. Playing football and hockey through high school, it was time to choose a sport, and a college. Having offers to play one or the other. I chose to take a scholarship and go play hockey at Colorado College, a Division One program with a lot of tradition. I spent my freshman year at CC, and then back in Minnesota for the summer. Right before my sophomore season started, my older brother who was in school at Arizona state was hit over the head with a 2x4 during frat fight, which split his skull, normally causing death. After three months in a coma, 2 more of bed-ridden sedation, and he was coming home; incapacitated with brain trauma, blind, couldn't feed himself, walk without assistance, talk, and he's being released from the hospital, heading back to back in Minneapolis with my recently divorced Mother.

It was a tough situation. I had a decision to make. I left my college scholarship, went home and brought my brother down to the brain trauma center every week at the University of Minnesota. Not sure what my plan was, I decided to enroll in school at Minnesota.

The following fall, I was offered the opportunity to jump in and fill a net on the JV hockey team. Having a body in front of the goal at the other end of the ice was much better than not, so they let me show up and practice. I was ineligible for 1/2 that year because of the transfer, so I spent time with family, going to school, practicing, and then playing some games on JV. One of the goalies on the Varsity broke his arm, I got called be the backup. The starting goalie faltered a little, I got a shot, strung together some wins and played regularly as we won the league and continued through the playoffs. I ended up starting the NCAA final-four that year, as a junior. It had been a long 2 years, early in my life. It's what I had always envisioned, perhaps more than I could have hoped for. Yet, in preparation, in diligent pursuit, when the opportunity came, the confidence was there because I believed, and kept moving forward. I learned a lesson of perseverance that has repeated itself several times during my journey.

My brother Mark lived another 21 years, with limited occupational capacity, blind, yet ever hopeful for the next day. He had an incredibly positive attitude and huge loving heart, which taught many of us big life lessons, before dying of complications from his injury. The homicide.

Exercise gratitude. Be curious. Care for and lift others. Occasionally pausing, keeping our eyes forward, constantly reflecting, we are able to see the brilliance in our experiences and the people around us. Know you are resilient. Keep persevering.

Personal growth is required for successful organizational change. When we embrace and engage people for who they are and where they are, each in their uniqueness, we strengthen the whole. We become better.

Change The Lens And Gain Perspective

An often-told story has stuck with me through the years and illustrates the fallacy of leadership myths. In a letter from Nathanael Greene to Nicholas Cooke in the spring following the infamous Revolutionary War battle at Trenton, where George Washington and his troops retreated across the Delaware River from New Jersey to Pennsylvania as the British kept decimating their numbers and their hopes, pushing them further west and near oblivion. They were all but beaten. Even Washington himself penned a letter prior to the December 26, 1776 surprise attack, saying he feared it may be game-over.

The men forced across that river were done, they'd suffered enough through repeated battlefield loses, loss of many friends and fellow soldiers; 90% of the army was gone, and many more had already called it quits and deserted. They were wounded, tattered without clothes and even shoes for some, out in the dead of winter with only days remaining in their enlistment, ending on January 1, and their leader is rallying to take them back east across that 300 yards of flowing ice. These were loyal men. They won that day in Trenton. These weren't trained soldiers, they were enlisted from the farm fields and towns and villages across the eastern scape, who we trying to care for their families and neighbors, and now they could fold and walk away honorably, having done more than could have been imagined. As they pushed south toward Princeton, a day away from the end of their commitment to the cause. Washington wasn't able to 'command' them any longer, so he bribed them with bonus wages to stay - not a single one accepted.

Then, as Greene shares with Cooke in his letter, Washington dejectedly rode off by himself for a period and when returning to his troops, made this appeal: "My brave fellows, you have done all I asked you to do and more than could be reasonable expected, but your country is at stake, your wives, your houses, and all that you hold dear. You have worn yourselves out with fatigues and hardships, but we know not how to spare you. If you will consent to stay one month longer, you will render that service to the cause of liberty, and to your country, which you can probably never do under any other circumstance."

As written by Adrian Gostick and Chester Elton, "The general went on to say he wished he could pass the burden of war to others, but there was no one to accept the charge. He urged the men to consider what they, and they only, could do. Asking them to think beyond themselves, to focus on the greater good, he promised them that if they would stay and fight with him, their glorious cause would change the world." One by one, they committed to stay.

Paraphrasing the great take-away in the following paragraphs from "The Orange Revolution," Elton and Gostick talk about the great lesson learned that day, and missing today in business. Above all, nothing "motivates like the opportunity to define and unite behind a common purpose... We simply don't know how to go about implementing a common direction... resulting in rivalries, turf wars, co-worker sabotage, and desertion, either physically or mentally... the cumulative costs for business are staggering." It's a great summation by Elton and Gostick in the context of their work on teams and culture.

The Believership lesson takes a look at this example from several different angles; Authority, duty, the figurehead leader, and self-belief/self-leadership of the individual.

It was the decision of each individual, for each other and their belief in a greater purpose that triumphed over despair, not the command of the leader. Washington's authority was null and void as the troops enlistment duty was expiring. Each man, individually took on self-leadership based on their own belief, exercised their personal leadership and then collectively band together.

Do It On Purpose

While not all the leaders talked about in this chapter overtly expressed their deep belief in the value of people, they acted on it. The result was extraordinary effort and commitment from their teams, and teams of teams. People found purpose and exercised choice. Believership was the superpower over any other form of motivation.

When our hearts and minds are connected in purpose, and we honor the commitment to others in our relationships, each individual excels, the teams thrive, and the company expands. Represent what you believe, operate with purpose, and act on those beliefs. The great mistake many leaders and their employees make is acting against their values and beliefs, doing as they are told, or feel obligated to do, for fear of losing what may not be worth having. The mental and emotional costs are high over time.

To help take your power back, shift your intent from 'what I have to keep' to 'what I have to give.' Holding on to something while sacrificing something greater is a decision based in scarcity and fear. When you are concern for others and aware of your gifts to give, your confidence rises, you're able to remain in a state of possibilities. You will help others. You'll lead.

Sacrifice some of your self so you can be filled with the joy and achievement of those around you. Get yourself out of the way. How many of us do that? Did we get up in the morning and spend the proper meditation time? Do we actively choose our mindset? Do we do the mental prep to achieve in manor aligned with our beliefs? Are we able to let go?

Be tenacious with personal development. Own it. We will struggle to create the best outcomes for ourselves and inspire belief in others without clear intention and diligent preparation. In this way you can walk strong in your belief and honor the fear and doubts of others. You're able to stay with them in the problem and consistently stay on point with the mission. You grow as you help others grow. This is not a hand holding exercise. The point is that when you meet them where they are, believe in them, honoring their sense of belonging and contribution, they become willing to move forward with commitment and resolve.

When we take ownership and responsibility for our personal development, it brings to focus the importance of continual growth, and the impact it has on our personal satisfaction. When that's aligned with the personal, team and company objectives, our engagement is full, active, purposeful, and our performance rises to new levels.

Tenacity fuels innovation, moves past the problem, always seeing the solution. It gives us vision to see the possibilities and outcomes and believe it is within reach.

I'll repeat the inspiring words from Nilofer Merchant, "Not everyone will, but anyone can."

Let Go. Lift Others.

Chapter 7:

Best Possibilities

Innovation is a discipline.

Leading through transformation is a discipline.

Transformation of our workplaces, our companies, and industries is underway. When something new is introduced that that threatens or replaces something old, it's been disrupted.

The available and critical choice to accept and move in this direction, and how quickly the choice is made, will determine future success or failure. If you're not changing, you're not growing. If you're not growing, you're standing still. Standing still in a rapidly changing business environment is dying, and dying is not a good condition for business.

Both, innovation and leading through transformation, require an exceptional combination skillset and mindset. Just as there is not one prototypical, best leader. There is not a one best method to solve problems and create positive change. However, this is certain:

Innovation and transformation are about people, not process.

Letting go of current state is the only way through to future state.

Nothing Will Flow From The Bottle With The Cork In It

We get in our own way.

Change can be hard, but it's more of a learned belief than reality. Change is the most natural rhythm in our lives, in our bodies, minds and nature. From birth though living, the seasons, weather, sunrise to sunset is in constant motion. We're programmed for change.

We've been told it's hard. Let's drop that myth. Yes, our personalities, environments, and experiences inform our degree of acceptance and willingness to change, but it happens with or without choice. We can choose to create change or have it happen to us.

We are in a new era, where resistance to change is not an option, actually we need to accelerate change by choice if we plan to set the direction for our business. To make it happen, human greatness is desperately needed.

We are operating in a new world of simultaneous disruptive forces:

- Five generations workforce for the first time ever, stretching the life & career stage norms
- Explosive technology transformation will continue to accelerate, causing new threats and creating new opportunities
- Innovative business model shifts are changing the landscape for companies, industries and global economies
- Demands of creating a more engaged and human experience for every employee are increasing, while our approaches to solve are stuck in reverse, and capacity is declining

Any one of these are significant disruptions. Combined, they can be overwhelming. Whole industries are fading and major entities disappearing. Intelligent, market-leading companies recognize these significant shifts and are acting to transform their business philosophy and culture, shifting the focus back to the most critical component – people.

There is still strong resistance from the rigid traditionalists. Unifying belief is fluid and rarely executed well. Theory without action is worth very little. We've become overly academic in our approach, pondering without cause, and assessing after the fact. Innovation is the discipline of discovery and imagination. It requires questioning. It's reliant on the discipline of making choices to discard something current, to implement something new.

To succeed, grow and sustain, companies need to re-imagine the operational theories and structures, with special attention on over-orchestration of process and labor, which were formed and dangerously rooted in the industrial bureaucracy, and then became the base for governance, compliance and policy. This foundation is the "cork in the bottle."

Innovation is the freedom of choice, dependent on the wisdom of letting go. The 'proven through time,' academic process of empirical proof is a backward lens of reflective analysis, not allowing experimentation, debate and exploration of the possible. We've killed our enthusiasm for creative solutions and stripped human ingenuity from our capabilities.

This regimented compliance to process-excellence holds back innovation and has become ubiquitously ingrained in the psyche of business. We adhere to our current belief based on out-of-date philosophies that the term 'best-practice' is spoken as a commanded statement of fact.

No other statement blocks innovation and progressive, positive change more than "best-practice. The simplest things, like tying laces on a shoe, don't have 'one-best-way' to do it. We select a preference, but there are options, and each option accomplishes the task.

Methods of Madness

As published in Popular Science, there are '177,147 Ways to Tie A Tie.' Mikael Vejdemo-Johansson, a mathematician in Stockholm, recently led a small team on a quest to discern how many tie knots are possible. Undoubtedly, you've been taught a "best-practice."

Over the years I have progressed from cringing, to laughter when I hear this term. It's brought joy to my life - I laugh often. With nearly a billion dollars in business experience, never, was a method or process relevant to success. They were often helpful, sometimes harmful, but never a cause for success or failure, and certainly never was a practice, best. In fact, dismissing this nonsense and managing to people's natural strengths was the magic of success.

Looking at the future of business, with unprecedented complexity and volatility, the greatest mistake we can make is to stifle human ingenuity. However, we seem committed to doing so with benighted resolve. In pursuit of control, and mechanization of human behavior, we've restricted our capacity to meet today's significant challenges in a time when we need to expand our human capacity, creativity, and ingenuity.

What I have experienced, and learned to be true, is given the opportunity, people will amaze us. We all can point to examples of innovative breakthroughs and incredible feats. Often these are divergent and counter-intuitive happenings. These disruptive forces are prevalent and escalating in our current business climate.

How do we react? By clinging to methods of madness.

There is a dozen predominate software development methods; many dozens of sales methodologies, and then the entanglement from a plethora of sales processes, complicated by tools to orchestrate and govern - it's a mess! HR has methods and best practices for every operational task. And, management methods? It's fair to enumerate them equivalent to the number of grad schools across the globe, interpreted and exacerbated within every training method and the thousands of consultancies.

We have far more options than the 177,147 ways to tie a tie, yet we command adherence to a preference, a selection from many possible choices. And we use it as a statement of fact - we tortuously hit people over the head with it many times a week, perhaps day.

The tie options pale in comparison to "Best Practices" in business.

Certainly not maniacal in intent as these evolved, but overtime have morphed into methods of obedience and control, becoming as restrictive as swimming with a jacket on; as practical as running a marathon in suit and tie, or pumps.

The current state of this long developing phenomenon has birthed the industry of certification, the ridiculous accreditation addiction that holds role-based hostages and creative oppression. We marvel at the unique gifts of the outliers, and the accomplishments of performance disciplines like theater, music and the arts, yet disallow, dismiss it in the business setting – adamant to make everyone the same.

What people are hungry for is freedom. Freedom of thought, creativity and honor of expression. Sensibility matters, feelings matter, and belonging is coveted over fit. Assimilation of thought and action is a restrictive barrier to achievement and growth for individuals and companies. Compliance and ethics are no longer burdensome impediments, we all see the need, it's a desired state of operation. It's this emergence of this cumbersome, artificial standardization, that is prohibiting innovation and evolution.

It is time to unleash potential and embrace vision for possibility.

This is an everyone game, and urgently needed, requiring substantial change. The best news of all, is that it simply depends on our ability let go of the unneeded, more than what needs to be created.

What we stop doing is more important that what we do next.

Can we open our minds, our hearts, and envision a purpose-driven future? Can we unchain ourselves from the over-orchestration and artificial barriers to empower us with the freedom to embrace the brilliant world of possibility?

Prescriptive Authority

Growth requires change and change is not a best practice.

On a recent trip, I overheard a conversation on the plane. I interpreted it as a 'boss' instructing her subordinate and it wasn't pretty. She was demanding the subject to follow the 'chain of command,' and make sure she knows everything, be the first informed, before anyone else, so she could position it right. Then the statement came, "we need to follow best-practices."

Apparently micro-management was in their company's "Best-Practice" manual. Control and belittlement were standard operating procedure.

Like water-torture, this phrase is used as a tool for control, clearly and repeatedly sending the message to comply with the way the person in charge wants it done. Good or bad, true or false, it's a best-practice, reliant on century old, 4-word strategy, "because I said so." I guarantee the merchandising, ecommerce and supply chain gurus at Toys R Us had best practices in place, that turned out to be not so good at all.

We have a pattern of denying what is possible – holding onto the past to avoid the pain of growth. We take on just enough responsibility to get the reward but not excited about the challenge and possibility of self-growth, instructing people just follow directions, just do the job.

The constant voice inside companies sounds like this:

It can't happen.

Everything is just fine!

Don't rock the boat. Then suddenly an outside market event tips the boat; an executive leaves the company, a major client evaporates, a forecast is off. These would be little issues compared to some of the world events we see each day, so thank goodness for small problems, yet they are issues that spark change. Whether we want it or not, expect it or don't, it happens every day.

Become Aware Of How It Is To See How It Can Be

How do we get there?

Every week someone tells me that all efforts of goodwill and belief in an evolved state of business that puts HumansFirst is doomed to failure until some government intervention or World Economic edict is pressed into action. I am told that until Fortune 100 CEOs have some epiphany that fundamentally alters their belief and actions, that no change is possible – that I am wasting my efforts and essentially talking nonsense.

Usually, it is an older man – who has apparently surrendered to the chains of despair, presenting their limiting beliefs as wisdom. I feel for them. It's a steep climb.

Capitulation is inversely related to strength of belief and determination. For me, it's not a matter of being right, it's a deep desire to become better, and belief in humanity. There is no illusion that this imperative evolution will happen in a single season, in rapid fashion. Nor do I hold any belief that some authoritative agency, or stroke of a manifest will accelerate or heighten the impact.

I believe in people. Business is people. When every emerging leader understands choice; every brilliant, vibrant rising professional from start-ups to big-4 consultancies, to global 1000 entities are aware of options, change will happen. Having access to alternative programs, teachings, groups of people available for relationships within the communities of HumansFirst advocates and practitioners, multitudes will make this decision and pursue this path.

Assimilation to "everybody or nobody" thinking is weakness. I dismiss the defeated voice of acquiescent elders, the cynics, the pontificators. I have zero confidence that archaic agencies can influence an edict. I do know that given the opportunity, people will amaze us. To move from how it is, to how it can be, determine if you're 'conducting' business, or 'creating' business. It takes divergent, creative thinking to bust through the status quo. Making a positive impact with creative thinking requires great awareness.

The opportunity to press forward with alternative selection; programs and education options, vast networks of heart-centered leaders, consultants, coaches, educators and peers that become the 1000 ramps and doorways to a better future. A sustainable, evolved and ultra-productive future.

Love is a business word. This is the first barrier, the first gate to pass through. It is an inside job – a shift from within, and confident pursuit of that intuitive urging. It will not, cannot be impressed upon us from the outside. Shed the false constraints, the battered voice of limiting beliefs and failed wills of the past. We need to explore alternatives. What can be done better rather than the same way?

Do we believe in what we are doing? Do we understand it? Are we giving it everything – growing personally and helping the other person to succeed? Do we have a sense that it all adds up, that we are vital to the whole and take responsibility?

Awareness requires constant attention. Conditions are deep and fluid. Self-check on your belief, your energy and the accountability of your actions.

Innovation Is About People And Communication

It starts with vision. Vision is a critical component to success; in fact, it defines success. A clear vision provides the basis for your everyday tasks and the roadmap for others to follow. The power of visioning is everywhere, for example, Henry Ford envisioned everyone owning a car; Bill Gates envisioned a computer in every home (he undershot this one); Musk saw a battery-operated luxury car; Bezos saw the future of ecommerce. Visioning is also used for environmental, societal initiatives, teams and individuals. The first steps of accomplishing something is to see it.

Doing things the way we do them, simply because that's how it has been done in the past, is weak minded and not worthy of your attention and energy. Allowing poor behavior to continue, or dragging outdated and "harmful" practices forward is ignorant and lazy. It's imperative we acknowledge truth.

Technology does not solve problems. Humans use technology as a tool and organizations must stop depending on it as an endpoint; as the driver rather than the vehicle. It is powerful in the facilitation of human ingenuity to achieve what can be envisioned, not the means to vision.

Current engagement and incentive programs are impersonal and non-inclusive. To empower human ingenuity and organizational innovation, these programs need to acknowledge and honor the unique journeys and perspectives of others, encouraging and rewarding growth rather than compliance and assimilation. Experience and knowledge build our beliefs over time. Constant challenge, learning and maturity are essential.

Where we are stuck, without vision, and failing to offer direction, is creating the employee experience that allows for personal goals to be obtained and accelerated personal growth to be encouraged and supported. We've invested so much time and money into a systems approach with a passing nod to some tweaks in perks and benefits, that the important stuff was completely missed. People operate through relationships.

Throughout time, we have always gathered and converted people to our cause. We build armies, we build teams, we build theoretical and philosophical followings – we always have – its human. In the business sense, for the past 6 decades, the workforce gathering practice has been based on promotion: "This is a great job – this is a great company – this is a great mission." We've been sold someone else's vision, not empowered to discover our own. What is changing all around us and we are having a difficult time reacting to is, the practice of promotion is morphing into the need for attraction. The old belief: "we have a job for you, and we will pay you," isn't a compelling proposition. Having a job, trading time for money, and committing without voice, without alignment to personal goals and values, being forced to adopt other's ambitions and beliefs, is not the end-all offer it used to be. People are thinking and acting with a greater consciousness and discernment. They need to believe.

Nothing is more critical to a team than camaraderie. Not the lunch and happy-hour stuff, not the picnic or bowling outing, those are fine but that's not the essence. The way people communicate, the ability to have open discussions and the rhythm of engagement are very important. To accelerate adoption of change, to innovate and succeed on transformation initiatives, and deliver on the company vision, this needs to significant adjustment, in belief and action.

Belonging is essential to our existence – our wellbeing. So why do we drastically miss this connection through our professional lives? We've been brain washed into process assimilation – sameness, where the individual is merely a cog in the process. We take our cues from technology implementers, losing connection through low value tech process; how we recruit, on-board, measure, track and monitor, surveying, etc. Research suggests that we use more technology, open more listening channels. No one is listening, because there is no communication. To solve engagement and improve the employee experience, we need to use the listening channels attached our heads.

Impersonal, detached process leads to detached employees. The problem is clear. The answer is simple. Unwind the decades of misguided programs. These have created the challenge. Conversation, human to human engagement, is the answer. This change of belief and approach is critical. We've become focused on internal tasks and lost our ability to see clearly ahead. We lack vision due to our reliance on execution excellence – process control over human capability.

Two fundamental elements to allow this transformation to occur are service and empathy.

Service is more than the acts we perform; it is a philosophy of human interaction. When we approach our relationships with the heart of service, we unlock the power of two, and allow this to multiply. We experience all things "greater than ourselves." It is abundance. Self-focus is operating in scarcity.

Empathy, as a default state, removes judgment. Through empathy we first respond to people with curiosity, who they are, what's their perspective, and honoring how we are different, therefore appreciating our commonality. Approaching people with empathy is inclusive rather than exclusive. IT breaks down walls and allows a better-together basis of engagement.

People need to be valued, able and encouraged to express ideas and contribute with confidence, void of ridicule. To be effective, an environment of psychological safety needs to exist. Self-actualization, accountability and a grip on emotional intelligence are required, along with a clear purpose and strong communication. Without consistency, led through a culture of Believership, it unravels fast.

To accomplish innovation, we must be reaching, always seeking improvement, and focused on the advancement of others, as well as ourselves. We must constantly learn.

The Paradox of Employee Engagement

Employee engagement is 100% the responsibility of the employee.

Providing an environment where that is possible, is 100% the responsibility of the company.

Employee engagement has become the problem we seemingly love to have. The numbers have continued to decline since 2005. Why are we going the wrong direction? We face a disconnect between expressed culture and experienced culture. Everyone is pontificating, applying more of the failed solutions and no one is taking responsibility.

Employee engagement is the responsibility of the employee because they are the ones driving their personal outcomes. They know their own satisfaction measures. They are in control of their personal growth. They choose their mindset, their attitudes, and how they show up every day. Therefore, each employee is responsible for their level of engagement, the energy they bring and how they engaged with others.

The flip side to that, *the responsibility of the company and HR leaders, is to provide an environment where personal growth is possible*, and that remains a disconnect. That is the fail point. When the employee takes responsibility for their own engagement, then you need to get out of their way. Hands off. Stop force feeding old ideas. Stop knowing better and limiting through narrow parameters.

We want people to be engaged with what we tell them to be engaged with. Traditionally, personal growth was mapped to the next slot on the org chart, and remains adherent to this limited, hierarchical belief pattern. That was good enough 20 years ago. Not today.

The ambitions, opportunities and incentive priorities have changed. Traditional thinking is locked into two factors – promotion and more money. That was simple. When a promotion or raise happened, companies could say, we are contributing to your personal growth. More often today, the employee is thinking, those aren't the measures of my personal growth. I have my own ideas. I know what I want to achieve, and the learning and development that you're offering me is not getting me where I want to go. I don't have the enjoyment, the passion, the satisfaction when I get up every day because you're forcing me into your way of thinking, your beliefs, and the corporate culture that I don't necessarily buy into. You're feeding me leftovers from long gone era.

Traditional Thinking Is The Barrier

Yes, this is a challenge. What is being done today does not solve the problem. Continuing current approaches will continue current results - engagement numbers drop - engagement numbers drop - engagement numbers drop.

This is a new and exciting era of business. The realities must be faced to experience the possibilities. The way people consume and engage with information, the expansiveness of ideas and opportunity has changed so dramatically over the last ten years, exceedingly more rapid over the last five years, and as that workforce continues constant interaction with expanding information, they become aware of options and make personal career decisions. The information they're consuming is not coming from your career map, perhaps not even from within the company. They're not dependent on their boss or the company to give them that fulfillment.

Therefore, the company must provide the environment for them to be fulfilled, to experience personal growth and align outcomes to values.

Listening And Learning

As I walked into a meeting at Microsoft, general conversations were taking place as everyone got situated. The leader entered the room and starts with a few funny jabs at a couple of people. Laughter breaks out and the whole dynamic for the meeting was set. It suddenly felt like a gathering of friends, not a dreaded business meeting. People were engaged with each other. That is the simple yet powerful magic of a high-achieving culture, where people are open and free to engage as themselves.

That genuine interaction is the goal. It happens because of the belief that the leader has established. Consistently setting then tone and demonstrating care for everyone in the room. It's safe place to be. With that environment, everyone can bring their best. Discussions are open and more gets done.

What you don't know will hurt you. What breaks down fast is when we assume that we are right and start down the path of influence and persuasion of others, without understanding other perspectives. Experiential differences must be embraced, and diversity of opinion leads to better decisions.

People experience the company through the people they engage with the most. While we attempt to pour culture equally through the organization from the top down, it must be re-energized within each subsection, each division, every team. When activated with the core of the company, throughout the organization, where team culture mirrors corporate culture, it becomes sustainable.

An engaged leader will have an engaged team. In this era of accelerating change and disruptive forces, the propensity for the leader to demonstrably exemplify personal development and growth is essential to lead their immediate team and influence other teams throughout the organization.

If my experience working in a company is orchestrated by a universal vision created from a theory and generically fed to the masses, it will not be adopted. It's too fluffy, non-participatory, more like a movie, not an interactive experience. Top performers will create the high-achieving environment and lift others, when the whole team is adherent to a grand vision. When not aligned, they will detach from the immediate needs of the core team – their level of commitment will be minimized, as they have an escape route, a safety net, an excuse to disassociate due to lack of clarity, generalize and ineffective communication, and no sense of Believership.

To become an innovative organization, we must move away from our biased experience and beliefs that have unnaturally been forced upon us, and focus on what's next. We are required to challenge historic patterns, dissect the strengths and flaws to understand the desired future state.

It becomes imperative to differentiate heritage from culture. And make new choices.

Lessons From Mergers And Acquisitions

Most acquisitions start with a belief that the combination will yield a multiple in value. Reality is, most have resulted in a fraction of the combined whole. Less than – not more than.

Depending on whose research you choose to rely on, mergers have a failure rate of anywhere between 60 and 80 percent. One KPMG study found that 83 percent of these deals hadn't boosted shareholder returns. And 52% failed to achieve the original combined value.

Arguably, if the leaders of more mergers and acquisitions envisioned the future realities of combining people and relational dependencies, rather than the much simpler assessment of finance and operations, they may flip this trend and win more than they lose. Way too much emphasis is placed on the strength and vision of the leader, and far too little placed on the contributing masses of people actually conducting the business.

Realizing that this a bold proposition, let me illustrate the point:

Visualize a pyramid with the CEO representing the pinnacle. In a transformation effort, the CEO is demanding that every person in the pyramid will willingly get on board, make changes personally and drive change through their teams. In a 50,000-person company, 49,999 people are going to be forced into new behaviors and learning. They are called to interpret, take direction and adjust. The plans call for the whole company to shift in uniform fashion. Never happens. The approach is always to force methods from past experience into the new environment. The starting point is already the breaking point. The new reality of the combined teams, operational methods, and culture requires new thinking.

If the leader is not doing the work to learn and adjust, to show the way of change, people will not follow. The personal reluctance of the executive to learn, adapt and change, becomes the personal reluctance of the 49,999. The pyramid doesn't move – in many cases, it starts to break apart.

The opportunity to advance the business from current state to desired state, is largely caused by adhering to the status quo and self-protection motives. Quickly, the frustrations and disbelief show up at every level of the organization, throughout the whole employee population. The innovators are creating communities of forged on the principle that the whole is greater than the parts and each part an essential contributor. The 'parts' are your people. The belief or disbelief, success of failure, will come from people, predominately based on the belief in the executive leaders, business unit, and team leaders. To achieve the multiple in value, focus must be on the people.

Best Possibilities

There is not a rewind button to the simpler industrial era of command and control. Management is a process, a skill perhaps, but not leadership in this technological era, where process will continue to become more automated. It is human relationships, human interaction that will fuel the successful companies over the next decade. This shift has happened and is accelerating. These are the companies that will innovate on demand and handle transformation with agility. Information is automated, Wisdom and belief are human.

To get there, companies must change their identification and selection process of leaders. If we do not break the patterns that have cause our leadership crisis, failure is certain. Creative, diverse and inclusive leaders need to emerge quickly in your company. Stop what you're doing now and pivot.

Invest in human development, allow choice and reduce the controls that limit human ingenuity. Turn off some systems and start having more conversations.

The philosophical shift is moving away from the mindset of "this entity," and focus on "THESE PEOPLE." It is not trite – it is not easy. The first priority is to strengthen each person, encouraging each person to strengthen their teammate, and then the groups they collaborate with, and eventually Believership with be in place, innovation will be possible, and the value of the greater whole can be realized.

Take the opportunity to renew the vision, heighten and strengthen the new possibilities. Accept or explore new methods, ideas and actions. Invite change. Assess and discard old beliefs. Adopt new beliefs and influences.

> *It is much more than what we accomplish, it's who we become along the journey.*

Chapter 8:

Lift Others

I start each day with a morning meditation focused on two words: Lift Others.

I end each day with a reflection: Is It Better.

Did I do something, help someone, listen, learn something? Was there a positive impact today?

It's been consistent practice. A discipline that started as a way to set intent. Remaining open to experience the opportunities each day will provide, and avoid just conducting the daily events, allows me to stay present in the day.

Greater Value In All

There is great joy in contributing to someone else's growth, belief in themselves and wellbeing. It is also incredibly rewarding and energizing to accomplish exceptional feats with others, as part of a team, a company, and as a leader.

Believership, the result of great leaders, is energized with the belief of possibilities. The belief that more can be accomplished, change is both necessary and possible, fulfillment lives in the greater value for all. It is a mindset of abundance, knowing that as we succeed, the more we can give. To reach higher levels of achievement, to innovate, there must be a purpose greater than ourselves.

Performing for the company can drive us to a degree, but accountability to, and belief in the people with us on the journey is a purpose greater than ourselves, that propels us to be our best.

We know that being of service is a great feeling. It can elevate our mood, create satisfaction and spark gratitude. Think about a giving moment, a charity, volunteering, a contribution or the simple act of helping someone in a random act of kindness. That elated sense of peace and joy comes from these acts of compassion for others.

Expand that to a greater sense – a daily mindset where our best efforts, our creative thoughts and our energy is directed at contributing to a greater whole, something or someone we believe in. This is an ever-present choice we can make every day.

Envisioning this choice, these acts, is the catalyst for sustained achievement and growth. You matter, we all matter – every day! People depend on us, we trust ourselves, and the focus shifts from introspection to outward purpose. It's powerful stuff.

Is this your daily experience? Can you get there? It takes time and diligent effort. With this focus and intent, you are creating a habit that will serve you well as a leader – likely beyond what you can imagine. Your choice to embrace this approach to your day, your work, your interactions with people needs to be continuous and sincere over an extended period. At some point, weeks or months from now, you'll realize that you have shifted your mindset and become a bigger contributor to a larger purpose. And others will believe in you.

This is the greatest value of a leader, nurturing the belief that people collectively can accomplish way more than anyone could possibly do on their own.

When you operate in-service to others, confidence soars because there is no apprehension, self-seeking fades away. Our objectives are clear, and the outcomes are purposeful, more predictable, and allow at a higher level of achievement. Self-doubt, over thinking, hesitancy and insecurities will disappear as the benefit of others becomes the primary concern. We find that this mindset presents itself in other areas of our lives and becomes a natural state.

Find joy in life's changes. Change is a stimulus. Transitions, how we respond and adjust to the change, can become an exciting and desirable pattern. As we truly focus on serving the greater whole, we develop a broader sense of self and become interested in the experiences and ideas of others. We adapt to change, seek growth, and naturally embrace empathy.

In The Path Of Others

If people aren't with you, believe in you, you're not leading. When people are with you, it's your responsibility to be with them, know their path, listen and understand. Strength grows as you exercise it, share it, which is the true strength of a leader.

Believership happens when we're able to unlock the hearts, minds and voices of those we are with. This is real strength. This is the future model of leadership.

Too common in our current business landscape, still operating with the restrictive leadership models, ideas and experiences are ignored or filtered, diminishing individual and team impact. The commanded orchestration of our operational processes has become bloated and generic, blocking out the value of human ingenuity, and clogging the natural flow of innovation and growth.

Honoring the responsibility for other's achievement, requires leaders to commit to people in a greater degree than they are expecting – exceedingly more than what has been taught in the past. Express and demonstrate belief and care for them first, and have the strength and wisdom to know it is returned and multiplied throughout the organization. When people believe the leader cares, they share that belief with others, strengthening commitment and return that belief to the leader and the greater whole.

Uniqueness and Innovation

We must break current patterns to immediately prepare people and organizations to innovate, navigate and create - the future is here. Tremendous shifts have already happened. If we stand firm in old patterns, while trying to assess and understand these new realities, we'll fall further behind. Another wave of change is occurring while companies wait, unwilling to let go – these are the companies shrinking, faltering, disappearing.

Positive change is not possible in the old industrial-era philosophies, adhering to belief in archetypal management and rigid operation processes. Those companies that value process over people, hierarchy over humanity will lose talent, and continue to struggle as they become further irrelevant and unattractive as a place to work and a place to invest. Many enlightened leaders and companies have already recognized this reality and have made this shift. And many more are turning in this direction. It's much more than a new wave of business philosophy, it's recognition of the necessity for survival.

While old patterns of leadership and operation will shrink or kill businesses, so will dependency on the advisory services that are equally reliant on, and beholden to the constraints of past models. Consultancies and support orgs struggling with the problem are unlikely to help their clients speed through the required change. New thinking, new programs and approaches are entirely required. These are not systemic program changes, they're human based, human empowering shifts that have been ignored and subdued through the long-time procurement, adoption and management of rigid processes and controls.

How we attract, select and engage employees is a key area of focus. New skills and expanded capacity are required, diametrically opposed to the standards of sameness and assimilation in place today. *PWC's 'Workforce of the future: The competing forces shaping 2030' clearly states the reality:* "We are living through a fundamental transformation in the way we work. Automation [is] replacing human tasks and jobs, and changing the skills that organizations are looking for in their people. These momentous changes raise huge organizational, talent and HR challenges – at a time when business leaders are already wrestling with unprecedented risks, disruption and political and societal upheaval.

The pace of change is accelerating. Competition for the right talent is fierce. And 'talent' no longer means the same as ten years ago; many of the roles, skills and job titles of tomorrow are unknown to us today. How can organizations prepare for a future that few of us can define? How will your talent needs change? How can you attract, keep and motivate the people you need? And what does all this mean for HR? This isn't a time to sit back and wait for events to unfold. To be prepared for the future you have to understand it."

Deloitte's 2019 Global Human Capital Trends report captures the recognition and scale of our challenge:

"Leading a social enterprise is about recognizing that, while businesses must generate a profit and deliver a return to shareholders, the must do so while also improving the lot of workers, customers, and the communities in which we live. And in today's world, with today's societal challenges, fulfilling this aim requires reinvention on a broad scale."

A fundamental shift in our thinking is critical to make progress, and we must consider a denied truth:

People are unique. Each individual has different gifts, and life experiences, according to their background and interest. For decades, companies have narrowed profiles down to exclude creativity, with an idealistic preference for a for a rigidly traditional path, pattern and skills. Believing they hired the best and brightest, they settled for the most alike. Organizations have therefore become one-dimensional in their thinking. It is painfully clear now that this is a detriment, not a strength. Going forward (I suggest starting today) companies need to abandon the profiles and avatars of the past and quickly identify what true innovative skills are, where these people can be found and how to attract them. Most importantly, they need to change the way they select and promote leaders, and abandon the industrial operating regimen. Business cannot re-invent doing the same things.

The term "fit" needs to die. No longer is a "good fit" desirable. 'Fit' needs to be replaced with "contribution" or "impact." Even more importantly, and likely more difficult, leaders, HR and talent acquisition has to change their *Beliefs*. Future employees, future leaders, will be valued on their natural gifts, not their surrender and adherence to a systems-driven world. If a person's gift is creative, then engage them to create; if it is to lead, then allow them to lead people aligned with their beliefs; if it is management, then give them process responsibility; if it is supporting, then give them freedom to support; if it is instructing, have them instruct. This not a game of compliance and capitulation. It is a movement of respect, empowerment and teaming. It is a significant change. Don't fool yourself that you're already there.

This new reality will naturally open your organization for diversity and inclusion, as the attraction and selection process become void the limiting profiling of the past. It requires throwing out (turning off or reconfiguring) decrepit systems and measures, and establishing more meaningful evaluations and methods.

More research help: "Against a backdrop of uncertainty, economic turmoil and unprecedented change a new picture is emerging of the skills and traits for success (and perhaps even simply survival) in the modern era. At the heart of this essential skillset for the future lies --creativity.

A raft of recent research studies demonstrates that creativity is vital from the shop-floor to the boardroom and at the level of the individual to the organization as a whole. What is more, our economic fortunes at a societal level probably rest on creativity too."

The Boston Consulting Group has been running an annual strategy survey for the last 8 years. For 7 out of 8 years creativity and innovation have been the top ranked strategic imperative. Hardly surprising - it is innovation and creativity that enable the development of new ways of working that ensure profitability.

IBM's global survey of 1500 CEOs found that creativity was considered to be the number 1 leadership trait for the future: *"more than rigor, management discipline, integrity or even vision - successfully navigating an increasingly complex world will require creativity."*

Why? "Leaders will need to be creative (solve problems in new and useful ways) to stay abreast of rapid change. Further, they will need to orchestrate and encourage creativity across all the levels, for which creativity is important. They will need to identify and develop creativity in individuals, build and nurture creativity in teams and set the culture and align processes to promulgate creativity throughout the whole organization."

I believe this to be true. Many years of leading through transformation has taught me this. Amazingly, denial and even harsh resistance remains steady, and while some adopt new language, they haven't changed procedures or beliefs. I'll repeat an earlier statement: You either create change or it happens to you.

Believership In Action

Since discovering the power of Believership three years ago, I've been on a mission to advance the great change needed to prepare organizations, leaders and teams for the future. The largest barrier is the industrial mindset - the greatest opportunity is to pivot with velocity to focus on people over process and raise human capacity. From transformation programs through large corporate M&A, to significant problem solving and the dynamics of high-achieving teams, my consulting has been focused on the human element in business. With a clear understanding of the need to emancipate people from the chronic and hardened quagmire of antiquated beliefs. I set out against the tide with strong belief in my experiences and in people.

While the steps forward are met with resistance, I've discovered cracks of enlightenment, progressive companies, and became aware of the escalating needs as I worked with teams and executives that we're struggling with high-function, much less high-achievement.

I've met amazing people aligned and active in this imperative shift. Knowing the strength of many working together, and a love for working in teams, I spent time and resources cultivating these relationships with a design on collaboration for greater and more rapid impact.

One strong, spiritual supporter was Claude Silver, Chief Heart Officer for VaynerMedia. She is the exemplary heart-centered leader needed for organizations to successfully usher in the new era. On a visit to NYC, we discussed ideas, experiences and our belief in possibilities for a significant awakening and transformation of leadership and corporate culture. Claude was living in this belief and making it real for VaynerX employees every day. Leading with heart, she was brilliantly sharing and teaching others, and establishing this belief throughout the organization.

Through Claude, I met Mark LeBusque, author of "Being Human," and we decided to get together and have a discussion on what it was like to be human in the workplace today while Mark was visiting from Australia. Jill Katz joined us, and the four us set a date and took a leap into an experiment, engaging an intimate group in open dialog about what people were experiencing in their workplaces.

As the planning started, I also reached out to others that inspired me, business leaders, authors, influencers who were advancing new ideas and innovative programs, each with varied perspectives and disciplines. We discussed ideas, the envisioned mission of HumansFirst and possibilities for positive change and began planning events in their cities following the NYC kickoff.

Envisioned as a program of conversation and discovery, this "anti-conventional" event-experience, sparked curiosity, attracted the interest of others, and brought more relationships. Slowly the group grew, awareness grew with each event, and a greater group of diverse change-makers joined in, more introductions spread, and more events were planned.

Amazingly, people started connecting from all over the world, curious, hungry for hope for the possibility of positive change, to make the shift away from the current state of affairs and break the chains of oppressive, toxic work environments and horrible leadership. The crisis is real. The pain is great. Through all of these discussions, embracing stories, ideas, desires and ambitions of the hundreds, then thousands, has accelerated the HumansFirst mission into a compelling global movement of like-hearted people who are full of hope and determination to bring about a better future.

In the first 11 months, this non-organization, self-funded "Club" has gathered people together in 10 cities, where experiences were shared, emotions and passion flowed, ideas were explored and people truly showed up for each other, expressing hope, compassion, programs and solutions. People from 20-70 years old, all genders, all races, from all levels of professional experiences continue to engage every week, from every continent, dozens of countries and hundreds of cities. HumansFirst has organically emerged as "place" where like-hearted humans from across can find each other, strengthen each other, share ideas, collaborate, come together and stand on common ground exploring with intent to ignite and accelerate a shift in business culture to value humans-first.

Together, we are seeing that we can raise the energy and impact of the kind and empathetic, the caring and giving, and bust down barriers and limitations of the past beliefs. As we unite in our bold belief of wellbeing for others, ourselves, our communities and workplaces, forward-thinking companies are stepping into the stream and engaging in new learning, new programs and re-imagining their beliefs and methods of operation. It is centered on an exceptional belief in human capacity and potential, fueled with optimism and curiosity, empowering continuous cultural transformation and business growth. For those without a voice this is an opportunity. For those with a voice it is a responsibility to lift others.

Every week more incredible leaders step forward. We are creating awareness and offerings to turn the tide and shift the focus to expanding human capacity, enabling organizations to become value creators rather than value extractors, and evolve our professional cultures, establish sustainable transformation and accelerated growth.

All of us are acutely aware of the challenges we face - with significant evidence, that the current state-of-affairs is neither desirable, nor sustainable.

With a belief that each us, each of you, is part of this solution. This global community of voluntary members continues to expand and support each other, embracing the challenges of transformation, celebrating our gifts, our diversity, our individuality.

To meet the growing demands and desires, the HumansFirst Playground, an opt-in community was created to connect and build relationships with others from around the world. Together we exercise our creativity, intuition and innovation, share our experiences, trials, and spark discovery through focused and open dialog. And inspire outcomes that raise achievement, fulfillment, growth and wellbeing as we solve today's biggest workforce challenges.

People know they belong here; they found a community where they can connect with others to learn and discover, infuse different ideas, spark deep and open conversation, and learn what is really going on in companies, what experience are people having, what are the central issues, so we can expedite corrective action.

Believe We Can

The research clearly points at the problem; value extraction, from humans and other resources by any means to maximize profit is not responsible or sustainable. CEOs are starting to realize they must do more than pass a memo to HR, who remain adherent to the advisement of technology vendors and college professors, and bring change throughout the organization through leaders in all business units.

To make it happen, make the shift to value creation, the Industrial mindset must be purged.

We have choices. We create or adopt patterns based on choice. The opportunity and challenge are to explore our beliefs at the root of our patterns. When we gain this clarity, we can make behavior shifts aligned with our beliefs and inspire better outcomes.

Rather than avoid conflict, interpreting it as a negative, we can embrace healthy conflict, the exploration of diverse ideals and experiences of others that challenge us to envision change. We choose to grow or remain chained to the status quo. To lift ourselves to the surface and separate from the current prohibitory environments. We are empowered with choice to create value each day, and change the hearts of the value extractors by demonstrating our beliefs.

As we lead, we are compelled to change the measure, change the equation of value from 'get more' to 'give more.' Ignite the path forward, becoming value creators rather than value extractors. Personal growth is required for successful organizational change.

When we embrace and engage everyone in their uniqueness, we strengthen the whole. Emotional intelligence, awareness and intent are key to leading through change.

We've been led to believe that change is hard. Positive change is uplifting and energizing. While the first steps may be bumpy, we soon realize that short lived transition has long-lasting benefit, in work and in life, and in this we are able to experience greater fulfillment and the ability to act on our purpose.

Rapidly expanding awareness is fueling demand for culture and leadership change. This acceleration is creating a clear vision of business winners and losers in the near future, where losers will continue to complain about generational differences, and talent wars, other such non-sense, while the winners – those that make the shift to putting HumansFirst - will experience the abundance of talent, ingenuity and diversity as they attract and engage their people through Belilevership.

You Have A Role And A Choice

Personal growth is required for successful organizational change. When we embrace and engage the whole person, everyone in their uniqueness, we strengthen the whole. Emotional intelligence, awareness and intent to lift others are key to leading through transformation.

I know it can appear a bit daunting, turning against the prevailing winds and moving forward. Studies help create some perspective. You're not alone in feeling the turbulence and doubt of change: The average person has 12,000 to 60,000 thoughts per day. 95% of those are the same as the day before, and 80% of those are negative. No wonder we get stuck in patterns. If this is comfortable, staying in this pattern because change is uncomfortable, then I certainly choose to become comfortable with discomfort.

We all worry. Think about what worries you. The vast majority of us (77%) worry about finance in our personal lives. Realistically, that percentage jumps at least 10 points in the corporate setting.

We worry about working more, our relationships, and whole bunch about performance measures (expectations and judgments of others), including grades, teams, college, job recognition/promotion. With this life-long, pressurized belief system, we focus on accumulation of status and things, often sacrificing our true potential as we assimilate to the perceived demands of others. We lose ourselves piece by piece, and in the end, we operate as someone we barely recognize. We have traded our core for external gain and that is a very telling scenario leading to bad behavior.

Our attitude is the greatest choice we make each day. This choice will build us up or break us down. To avoid allowing other's attitudes to break you down, find your self-leadership, your core beliefs, and choose well. We can prepare. We can plan for how people will react to us, or we can teach how to better interact, with appreciation and understanding of our dependencies.

We choose our outcomes. Yes, we respond to conditions surrounding us and actions of others, but fundamentally, we have the power of choice. Great change comes from the inside - then out. Be the best version of you today against any backdrop, within any scenario. Grow wise, stand strong, and put your beliefs into action with intent – create rather than respond.

Exceed limitations of the past and seek exceptions. When you become focused on growth, change is an enjoyable event. Always be a learner, always becoming. Believe and engage in something beyond yourself. Commit to connect and build relationships with the intent to Lift Others, therefore lifting all humanity, and every day you'll make a positive impact on your environment, culture and lives of those around you. Put love into action. Believe in yourself. Believe in others. Believe in a better future. Believership is the Super power Beyond Leadership.

References

The Boston Consulting Group annual strategy survey

2009 NESTA Everyday Innovation survey

Baer & Oldham, 2006 ; Frymire, 2006; Bottani (2010)

IBM global survey of 1500 CEO's

2010 Winning Ingredients report from Standard Chartered

Nilofer Merchant: Onlyness

Kimberly Davis: Brave Leadership

Toxic Workers Michael Housman Cornerstone OnDemand Dylan Minor Harvard Business School -Working Paper 16-057 Copyright © 2015 by Michael Housman and Dylan Minor

Jony Ive *(2013)*

Satya Nadella: Hit Refresh

Gallop: State of the American Workplace

Heather Hanson Wickman: Evolved Executive

Jeffrey Pfeffer: Dying For A Paycheck

Why Do So Many Incompetent Men Become Leaders: Tomas Chamorro-Premuzic

PWC: Workforce of the Future, Competing Forces Shaping 2030

Josh Bersin: Article 12/18/2018

Bloomberg BNA: HR Department Benchmarks and Analysis

Hilton Barbour: Hilton Barbour.com Blog

Earnst & Young Management Report 2017

Adrian Gostick and Chester Elton: The Orange Revolution

Robert K. Greenleaf: Servant Leadership, A Journey into the Nature of Legitimate Power and Greatness

The Evolution of Management Thought: Daniel Wren and Arthur Bedeian

Review of Classical Management Theories: Ziarab Mahmood, Muhammad Basharat, Zahid Bashir

Shawn Achor: The Happiness Advantage

Acknowledgements

With gratitude and appreciation for the Presenting Members, speakers, of HumansFirst. (listed by event city)

New York City:

Claude Silver, Chief Heart Officer, VaynerMedia:

I'm an emotional optimist, coach, manager, and mentor. As the first ever Chief Heart Officer it is my great honor to lead at VaynerMedia. I work for 800 Humans, and I am in touch with the heartbeat of every single person in the company. My role is to infuse the Agency with Empathy. It's my purpose. Culture is a texture. It's a vibe. A feel. And culture is alive. It's definitely not one or two-dimensional—I think culture is very three-dimensional. Culture is, in a nutshell, the heartbeat for me. It is something that absolutely lights up an entire system — if it is in place, and if it is thriving.

Mark LeBusque:
Provocateur, Author of "Being Human

I believe that starting with Human Being creates more Human Doing and that Every Human Being Needs to Belong. marklebusque.com was born from 25+ years of working in environments where good work had the potential to become great work but something was missing. The missing ingredient was the addition of a real human element where belonging and purpose intersected with the truth and authenticity. This ingredient sits within all of us however few add it to the recipe and fail to realize their true potential. It is my belief that in order to make real progress then humans must be able to speak their truth without fear or favor. My work helps humans to do this and organizations to embrace a more authentic way of being in order for the doing to occur.

Jill Katz: Founder and CHRO, Assemble HR: Influencer, Coach and Speaker who is passionate about shifting the workplace to be more #PeopleFocused. Using her "3C's" approach, #CandorCourageAndCare, Jill helps leaders and teams build a #WorkplaceThatWorks through Organizational Transformation, Candid Communication, Cultivation of Top Talent, and focus on Culture.

Seattle:

Heather Younger, J.D., CCXP:

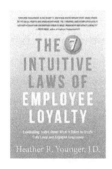

Heather Younger gets it. As a best-selling author, international speaker, podcast host, facilitator and coach, she has earned her reputation as "The Employee Whisperer". Her experiences as a CEO, entrepreneur, manager, attorney, writer, coach, listener, speaker, collaborator and mother all lend themselves to a laser-focused clarity into what makes employees of organizations and companies – large and small – tick. Heather has facilitated more than 350 workshops, reaching +1,000 employers and their employees. Her motivation and philosophy has reached more than 10,000 attendees at her speaking engagements on large and small stages. Companies have charted their future course based on her leading more than 100 focus groups. In addition, she has helped companies see double-digit employee engagement score increases through implementation of her laws and philosophies. She has driven results in a multitude of industries, including banking, oil & gas, construction, energy, and federal and local government. Heather brings a tenacious and humorous outlook to issues plaguing the workforces of today.

Her book "The 7 Intuitive Laws of Employee Loyalty" hit Forbes Must-Read list and is a go-to source for HR professionals seeking insight into their organization's' dynamics.

Heather's writing can also be found on her blog at CustomerFanatix.com, as well as articles in the Huffington Post, Thrive Global, American Express Open Forum, Tandem Seven, I Want It Now, and more. Coupled with her leadership podcast, weekly videos and employer newsletters, Heather stays connected to organizations long after she leaves the stage or conference room. When all the emails are returned and the mic is turned off, Heather acts as co-manager of her busy household in Aurora, Colorado with her husband, where they oversee their four children.

Turi Widsteen: Microsoft, General Manager Commercial Communications

Paul Haury

I am a <u>coach</u> and evangelist for heart based leading and culture, and creating workplace happiness. Our emotions either accelerate or inhibit our efforts, so, I encourage leaders, teams and individuals to go straight to the heart first. Happy people who care for each other outperform those that don't. In my pursuits, I do my best to be a learn-it-all for what motivates people in how they can be better for themselves, with each other, and, to make their world a better place. Over the last 25 years in education and work, I've had the wonderful fortune of people sharing their incredible hearts and skills with me. This allowed me to develop abilities where I love to help others with People Operations, International HR, Company Culture, Employee Engagement, Behavioral Social, Psychological and Neurological Sciences, Leadership Development, Agile, Lean, TQM and Teaching.

Renée Smith

Renée Smith serves as the Director of Workplace Transformation for Washington State as part of the Governor's Results Washington Team. She champions a more humane and effective workplace through primary research, writing, and speaking on <u>Making Work More Human</u> by increasing love and decreasing fear in the workplace. Renée leads the development of the Human Workplace community across the state and of resources for leaders, teams, and Lean advisers. Before joining Results Washington, Renée spent nearly seven years at the Department of Enterprise Services where she served on the Corporate Council and led the Organization Development Services Division that provided Lean Transformation Services and Change Excellence Services to DES and G2G Lean Consulting to other state and local governments. Renée earned a Master of Science in Organization Development from Pepperdine University. She was a 2014 recipient of the Governor's Leadership in Management Award for her original strategy work and Lean culture work at DES. She lives in a 102 year old Craftsman home in Tacoma and enjoys drawing for pleasure, cooking for friends and family, and exploring foreign cities

Dallas:

Kimberly Davis: Best Selling Author of BRAVE LEADERSHIP; Leadership Educator, cultivating confident, authentic, and powerful leaders

An expert on authentic leadership, Kimberly Davis shares her inspirational message of personal power, responsibility, and impact with organizations across the country and teaches leadership programs world-wide; most notably, her program "<u>OnStage Leadership</u>" which runs in NYC and Dallas, TX. Additionally, Kimberly teaches Authentic Influence and Executive Presence for Southern Methodist University's (SMU) Cox School of Business' Executive Education Program, and partners with SMU in teaching for the Bush Institute's Women's Initiative Fellowship program (empowering female leaders from the middle east) and for the National Hispanic Corporate Council. Kimberly is a <u>TEDx</u> speaker and her new book, *Brave Leadership: Unleash Your Most*

Confident, Authentic, and Powerful Self to Get the Results You Need, which has been named as the number one book to read in Inc. Magazine's "The 12 Most Impactful Books to Read in 2018," with a cover-endorsement by best-selling author Daniel Pink, is available at all on-line and brick-and-mortar bookstores everywhere.

Ozlem Brooke Erol: International Consultant and Speaker, Author of #1 Bestseller, Chief Purpose Officer

Purpose is a way of living, bringing more meaning to our lives knowing we are not here only for the daily grind. As Purpose-Driven Leaders we can touch people's lives in the most impactful and heart-centered ways and leave a long lasting legacy. Brooke O. Erol is one of the co-authors of the #1 International Best Seller *From Hierarchy to High Performance*. She is the Founder of two businesses, YourBestLife and Purposeful Business. She works with leaders, founders, C-level executives to create human-centered work environments where engagement improves and turnover is minimal. She is also an author of *Create a Life You Love*. She speaks internationally about Future of Work, Purpose-Driven Life and Organizations and Purpose-Driven Leadership.

Jason Croft: Credibility Craftsman, Owner of Croft Media and The Jason Croft Show

Jason Croft is a media strategist with a specialty in corporate podcast creation and video marketing. Connecting is at the core of everything he does. Connecting to other people, connecting people to each other, connecting people to ideas, and connecting businesses to their target clients. With his company, Croft Media, a B2B Media Agency, he creates 90 Day Authority Playbook Videos and Sales Funnel

Podcasts for his consultant and other solo-preneur clients. The former VP of Sales and Marketing at Magic Production Group, Jason produced and hosted over 80 episodes of *Startup Dallas*, a YouTube and iTunes series where he interviewed some of the most innovative CEOs and Founders in the Dallas/Fort Worth startup world. Now that he's running his own video marketing firm, he has his YouTube series, *The Jason Croft Show*. With it, Croft takes the same approach of in-depth interviewing of his guests that he's become known for and adds a twist of fun – setting each episode in a moving vehicle and finding out what really drives them. Jason loves his amazing wife and three boys, has a blast traveling around the world and often gets too close to exotic animals. He's been on icebergs and mountains, kissed and wrestled with black bears (pictures upon request), and even swam with a shark (not by choice!).

Mark Nagel: Senior Manager People, HR Transformation and Employee Services at Southwest Airlines

Mark Nagel currently is a Sr Leader in the People Department (Human Resources) at Southwest Airlines leading a special focus on HR Transformation and HR Technologies. Prior to Southwest Airlines Mark was a HR Director Best Buy for 15 years, covering a variety of HR operational areas including Affirmative Action, HR compliance and Employee Relations. In his spare time Mark serves on the Board of Directors and sings in Resounding Harmony, a non-profit chorus that performs concerts for other non-profits, raising funds and awareness for their causes. He also serves as Vice President of the North Texas Industry Liaison Group- an organization that helps federal contractors share best practices in Affirmative Action.

Denver:

Heather Younger

Heather Hanson Wickman, PhD: Author of Evolved Executive; The Future Of Work Is Love In Action

Today's forward-thinking leaders know that the future of work is human. It's about catalyzing people in pursuit of a meaningful mission. By leading organizations with soul, purpose and love, Heather Hanson Wickman, PhD, author of *Evolved Executive*, believes that conscious leaders can heal the crisis of suffering that's present in so many organizations and revitalize the workforce through innovative practices and deep self-awareness. Heather is a former healthcare executive, and in this episode, she offers insights, practical advice and invaluable strategies that allow leaders to reenergize your organization's purpose, enhance employee engagement and experience, develop a purpose-centered strategy in culture and lead from love instead of fear. As Founder of Untethered Consulting, Heather brings 10+ years of organization development consulting, both as an internal and external consultant. Heather has a bachelor's degree in Human Resource Development, a Master's degree in Human Resources/Industrial Relations, and a PhD in Organizational Systems with an emphasis in leading transformational change. Heather has incredible passion for supporting individuals and organization through positive change. Through her well established organizational experience, she has witnessed profound individual success and organizational progress. Heather is also passionate about research and writing. With several publications and co-edited books in circulation, she is continuously working on expanding and sharing an important knowledge base to help create organizational health.

Marcus Aurelius Anderson

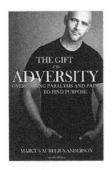

Marcus is a prolific speaker and thought leader, bringing a new voice to a generation desperately seeking understanding, perspective, and wisdom. His keynotes have been forged by the fire of experience, giving Marcus the unique opportunity to translate life's toughest problems into practical applications. His insight is universal, allowing him to reach across a multitude of demographics. A few of his key notes include The Gift of Adversity, Innovative Leadership, and Functional Philosophy. Buckle up for a story a lifetime in the making. The Gift of Adversity is Marcus' own personal journey through a life changing injury that left him paralyzed from the neck down. Suffering is a motif we can all relate to; but the timeless lessons learned and applied in realtime will leave you inspired to take advantage of the mindhacks Marcus discovered while in the midst of Adversity. The only way to cultivate better employees is to be a better leader. We often think of business as a pyramid, but the truth is as a supervisor we need to be the foundation and example of personal and professional development. Experience the dialogue of modern stoicism, Zen, and other warrior mindsets and unlock the secret to applying them to everyday life and business.

Los Angeles: Julie Winkle Guilioni, C0-founder & Principle, DesignArounds, and Best-selling Author

Julie Winkle Giulioni has spent the past 25 years improving performance through learning. She's partnered with hundreds of organizations to develop and deploy innovative leadership training solutions that are in use worldwide. Prior to co-founding DesignArounds 15 years ago, Julie was director of product development for AchieveGlobal, one of the world's largest commercial training companies. She also held multiple training leadership roles and was a department chair and professor at the Southern California university. Julie was named one of Inc. Magazines top 100 leadership speakers and received the Global HR Excellence Award for Strategic Leadership from the World HR Congress earlier this year. She is the co-author of the Amazon and Washington Post bestseller, Help Them Grow or Watch Them Go: Career Conversations Employees Want, a respected speaker on a variety of topics, and a regular contributor to many business publications.

Marcel Schwantes: Speaker, Leadership Coach and Consultant

Marcel Schwantes is a keynote speaker, entrepreneur, executive coach, and syndicated columnist attracting over 1.5 million visitors monthly to his thought-leadership. His work and writing has been featured on Inc., Time, Business Insider, Fast Company, CNBC, Forbes, Thrive Global, Medium and countless other news sites. Marcel speaks passionately on the human side of work, and how "love in action" is the machine that powers teams, cultures and whole organizations to thrive and outperform the competition. His company, Leadership from the Core, has positioned itself as front-runners in developing human-centered leadership-training programs founded on principles of servant leadership and actionable love.

Amy Blaschka: Co-Founder, Park City Think Tank

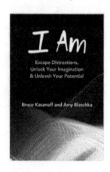

Amy Blaschka is the co-founder of Park City Think Tank, which helps leaders stand out for the positive in a proactive and vocal way. A frequent speaker and workshop leader, she studies, teaches, and practices positive, genuine communications. Amy serves as a ghostwriter/coach, helping her clients communicate effectively and focus on what—and who—matters most. She is also one of the most positive and popular storytellers on social media, whose engaging communication style has earned her an enthusiastic following. A former branding consultant, Amy helps accomplished professionals position themselves as thought leaders and communicate in a manner that enhances their connection with others. She covers "personal transformation and its impact on career growth" for Forbes.com and is the co-author with Bruce Kasanoff of *I Am: Escape Distractions, Unlock Your Imagination & Unleash Your Potential.*

Chattanooga:

Claude Silver, Marcel Schwantes

Jacqueline Jenkins, PhD, Chief Impact & Strategy Officer at United Way of New York City

Jackie is a sought after and highly visible leader, creative positive change across the globe. Her thoughtful and passionate advocacy is changing lives and elevating organizations into the future of work. She works closely with the executive leadership teams in the greater business community, and at the United Way organization and other stakeholders, leading strategy development, manage strategy execution, envisioning innovation and delivering against goals during a significant period of transformation at the organization. She is a masterful change facilitator and coach to individuals and teams in and outside of the workplace, and frequently collaborates with thought leaders in urban education, philanthropy, and organizational development and design.

Kevin Monroe: Founder, X Factor Consulting, Host of Higher Purpose Podcast

Business can be a force for good. I'm wired for purpose. And, purpose is the lens through which I view the world. I believe Purpose is transforming the world of work and business, in fact, I host an entire podcast exploring this topic. Those leading the way are purpose-powered, people-focused, and values-based. I partner with CEOs to create world-class workplace cultures that maximize employee flourishing and fulfillment. These workplaces welcome love and eliminate fear. I operate at the intersection of faith, business, and purpose. My desire is to do work that is truly transformational in its impact. My experiences in ministry provide me with an ability to do soul care for the people I serve. My experiences in business allow him to connect to businesspeople in a way that understands the challenges of business and relate to the pressures you face as a business owner. As a practitioner of Servant Leadership and Appreciative Inquiry, I seek to understand what it is that you want to accomplish and work collaboratively to co-create amazing results.

Charlotte:

Kimberly Davis

Dr. Melissa Hughes, PhD, President and Founder of The Andrick Group,

Author "Happier Hour with Einstein

 Melissa specializes in employee engagement, effective communication strategies, and the unique dynamics of the multi-generational workforce. Having worked with learners from the classroom to the boardroom, she incorporates brain-based research, humor, and practical strategies that impact how we think, learn, communicate, collaborate, and solve problems. Melissa helps educators and leaders apply neuroscience to build intellectual capacity and create a more engaged culture of learning and leadership. Her second book, "Happier Hour with Einstein: Another Round" is an expansion of the original book, "Happy Hour with Einstein," designed to illuminate those factors which impede or enhance learning, creativity, communication and collaboration for greater understanding of how the brain works and how to make it work better. Happier Hour with Einstein is a fascinating collection of neuroscientific discoveries and studies that explain how the human

brain manages our experiences, knowledge, emotions, decisions, achievements, and failures which shape the mental models we create for ourselves and the world around us. Why do we make irrational decisions or jump to illogical conclusions? Why do some people avoid challenges while others embrace them? Why does rejection hurt so much? Why does laughter feel so good? How does failure make us smarter? Why are optimists more successful than pessimists? Armed with advanced technology, scientists have discovered the answers to these questions and additional explanations about how we learn and think.

Karima Mariama-Arthur, Esq: Attorney, Author, Advisor, Leadership Development and Organizational Performance Management

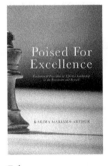

I am the author of 'Poised for Excellence: Fundamental Principles of Effective Leadership in the Boardroom and Beyond' (Palgrave Macmillan)–a provocative guidebook on leadership effectiveness. As a seasoned attorney, author, international keynote speaker, expert facilitator, complex communication consultant, and strategic leadership and management advisor, I have a proven track record for helping clients to raise the bar on achievement. I speak regularly before global audiences and provide unique insights that drive results. My shrewd ability to identify nuances helps clients to: → Establish credibility → Leverage expertise and → Build polished and powerful professional brands. With over two decades of multi-faceted legal, academic, corporate, and executive development experience, I have developed an extremely keen eye for the 'devil in the details' and am highly skilled at helping clients to leverage skills and talent across industries. Teaching clients to cultivate their Executive Celebrity™, I create specialized content for individuals and organizations using the principles, practices, and strategies that yield measurable results.

Washington DC:

Karima Mariama-Arthur

**Michelle L. Maldonado, MC-EICC, CMT-P:
Human Potential, EI and Mindful Business
Transformation, Compassionate Leadership,
Teacher/Facilitator, Keynote Speaker**

Michelle is Founder & CEO of Lucenscia, a human potential and mindful business transformation firm dedicated to developing leaders and organizations with positive impact in the world. She is leadership faculty for 1440 Multiversity and faculty and Meta-Coach for Dan Goleman's Emotional and Social Intelligence Coaching Certification program. Also a Certified Genos International Emotional Intelligence Practitioner®, Michelle is one of a handful of the Google-inspired Search Inside Yourself (SIY) Level 2 Certified Teachers® in the world and a True North Leadership Teaching Fellow. Michelle is passionate about helping create the conditions for a more connected and compassionate world by helping people do their inner work for outer impact. She has worked with Fortune 500 companies and organizations around the world to integrate empathy and compassion with resilience and high performance. A few organizations with whom Michelle has worked include LinkedIn, Microsoft, Dell, Capital One, Pfizer (Canada) and Deustche Telekom (Germany). Academic and government organizations include the National University of Singapore, New York University, Bay Path University, York Region (Canada) Government and Law Enforcement, and the Departments of Defense and Homeland Security. In recognition for her work on leadership and organizational development at the intersection of emotional intelligence, mindfulness, performance impact and compassion, Michelle was named "Top Corporate Leader" by HR.com's Leadership Essentials and "Woman of The Year" by the National Association of Professional Women. As a recommended speaker in SHRM's Speaker's Bureau, her work has been featured across industry publications and conference venues including The Mindful Leadership Summit, Training, Leadership Excellence, Human Capital Institute, the Institute for

Organizational Mindfulness and Chief Learning Officer. Michelle is a graduate of Barnard College at Columbia University, The George Washington University Law School and lives in the Washington, DC metropolitan area with her family.

Jackie Kindall: Founder of Kindall Evolve, Organization Success Catalyst and Leadership Transformation Expert, Executive Coach

I thrive on helping others grow and reach their goals. This applies not only to clients, but to friends, family and colleagues. Fortunately, I have shaped this innate drive which gives me sheer joy into meaningful work. In 2016, I founded Kindall Evolve Consulting, LLC after working in the Human Resources and Organization Development field for 25+ years. I work with leaders and organizations who are interested in building new skills, improving performance and getting results. As such, I have partnered with clients in a number of key areas, including:

- coaching leaders and executives to reach their goals, improve their performance, make lasting behavior changes, etc.
- designing and facilitating leadership development workshops to grow leaders who are effective at leading teams, communicating, managing conflict, leading with emotional intelligence, managing change, improving team dynamics, etc.
- designing and facilitating professional/team development workshops to improve team dynamics and team effectiveness
- planning and facilitating off-sites and retreats to create synergies, develop strategy, build teams, improve organization culture, etc.
- providing organization development consulting so that all aspects of the organization are aligned. I am passionate about helping leaders lead with emotional intelligence. This has a significant impact on leadership effectiveness, employee engagement and organizational culture.

> I support my clients by ensuring that they have the necessary tools to build amazing teams and thrive.

Brian Kelly, ACC, SSCC: Success Coach, Consultant, Human Development, Team Performance, Career Transition, Advancing Diversity and Inclusion

Brian Kelly Leadership Coaching offers human development and performance solutions to shift up your relationships and business results. Brian works with inclusive business leaders and their teams to grow their leadership effectiveness, human AND business performance. For our coaching clients, typical goals include: career clarity, career transition, leadership development, developing diverse leaders and teams, greater work joy, higher performance and better relationships. For our consulting clients, typical goals include: business growth, increasing team/organizational effectiveness, leadership pipeline development, organizational development and creating more human workplaces. Be Bold. Be You. Breakthrough.℠

Mali Phonpadith: Founder/CEO, SOAR Community Network, #1 International Best Selling Author, TEDx Speaker, Cofounder of SC Nebula

Mali Phonpadith is the Founder/CEO of the SOAR Community Network, TEDx Speaker, #1 International Bestselling author, marketing strategist, podcaster and the Executive Producer/Host of Tea with Mali TV Show. SCN is a strategic communications and talent management firm that supports Conscious Leaders and their businesses/organizations to spread their mission and create social impact. In 2015, Mali was selected as a Belief Team community partner for the Oprah Winfrey's

OWN Network BELIEF initiative. She has been nominated for several awards including Heroines of Washington D.C. Award by the March of Dimes and twice for the Women of the Year Award by NEW – Network Executive Women. She was awarded the iBoss Navigator award in 2018 for her work in helping small businesses message their mission and soar to success. She is a community champion for several local non-profits. She is the Founder of the SOAR Community Summit and producer/host of the SOAR Community Podcast. Mali is a four-time author, including A Million Fireflies, her memoir about her voyage from war-torn Laos to America. She is also the coauthor of Seen and Sustained: Best Practices in Communication that Increase the Visibility of Small and Diverse Businesses, a professional workbook for small businesses. In 2017, Born to Be Me, a compilation of authentic stories from 19 international female authors, made Amazon's #1 International Bestseller List. In 2018, The Balancing Act also made the #1 International Bestseller List. She has shared her insights at The Library of Congress, Smithsonian, University of Maryland, George Mason University, SAIC and other national venues. Huffington Post, Entrepreneur.com, Better Business Bureau (BBB) Trusted Magazine, BBB Podcast, Advisor Today Magazine, Asian Fortune Newspaper, WJLA DC, Radio Free Asia, WHUR Radio, Voice of America, and numerous blog talk radio programs.

Jessica Du Bois: Employee Benefits Consultant | Passion for 'Your" People, I connect Employee Experience with Healthcare & Benefits

Jessica Du Bois works with companies to modernize their employee benefits by focusing on employee experience and cost containment strategies. She is passionate about helping organizations prosper and attract top talent by focusing on their 'humans first'. Jessica is passionate about enhancing the workplace through making the difficult workplace topics such as mental and physical health easier to navigate through. Jessica is a consultant with Business Benefits Group and has been named a Face of Change in the benefits industry by BenefitsPro magazine. Find out more at https://jessicadubois.co.

Indianapolis:

Jason Barnaby: Tribe Leader and Chief Fire Starter, Fire Starters Inc.; Author of "Igniting the Fire Starter Within"

Jason Barnaby specializes in igniting sustainable change in individuals and corporations. A 20-year veteran of the adult education world, he has taught in Poland at WSB-NLU and stateside at IUPUI and DeVry. He worked for 10 years in the financial services industry in several roles including L and D, internal and external sales, HR and Transformation. In 2017 he founded Fire Starters Inc where he serves as Tribe Leader and Chief Fire Starter. The mission of Fire Starters Inc. is to work with individuals and corporations as they challenge the barriers of fear, build a tribe of supporters and find success in their original design. His first book, Igniting The Fire Starter Within, chronicles the lives of 5 Fire Starters who pushed past fear to live daily putting passion to purpose. The book is due out in January 2019. Outside of professional pursuits he is a devoted husband of 21 years, a proud father of 3, a distance runner and guitar playing singer/songwriter.

Dr. Katrenia Reed Hughes: Indiana University, Purdue University – Indianapolis, Assistant Professor of Organizational Leadership, Purdue School of Engineering and Technology

Dr. Katrenia Reed Hughes, known by her students and clients as "Dr. K," has a doctor of psychology (Psy.D) degree from Indiana State University, and a master's degree in business administration in leadership from Butler University. She is an assistant professor of organizational leadership in Purdue's School of Engineering and Technology at IUPUI. Her life mission is to help others put their passion to purpose. Her consulting firm, Passion2Purpose, LLC, provides STEM program evaluation, project management team-formation consulting, executive coaching, team development, performance assessment and strategic planning offerings. Dr. Reed Hughes is also available as a keynote speaker. Whether functioning in the role of teacher, therapist, consultant, facilitator, change agent, trusted advisor, project manager, performance coach or colleague, her primary motivation remains constant. She meets people where they are to help them articulate and realize their goals. Dr. Reed Hughes' view of learning to successfully address life's challenges is inspired by Nelson Mandela's words, "It always seems impossible until it's done." In her most recent corporate role, she was an enterprise learning and development partner at OneAmerica in Indianapolis, Indiana. She has over a decade of experience teaching college students and 10 years working in corporate organizational development. While at Indiana State University, she had an opportunity to teach undergraduate psychology courses including abnormal psychology and human sexuality. Serving as the human sexuality course coordinator, she led a team of graduate teaching fellows. Her passion for teaching was recognized with an Educational Excellence Award in the College of Arts and Sciences at Indiana State University. Dr. Reed Hughes enjoys being in the classroom and engaging with students outside of the classroom to advise and build confidence through the application of learning. Her background in psychology has served her well when it comes to building rapport with students from diverse backgrounds.

Isabel Hundt: Inspirational Speaker, Sociologist, The Leader's Heart Decoder, YA Advocate, Author

Isabel's journey started with a prophetic dream at the age of twelve. The German native tackled many obstacles in order to make her dream of speaking in front of thousands (in English) become a reality. Her biggest obstacle was learning to connect deeply with her Soul and her heart and to fully accept herself and her unique gifts as an Empath-Warrior™. She experienced rejection and betrayal, life-altering "failures", and depression and anxiety. Isabel's life is a beautiful reflection of how anyone can create a deep spiritual connection within themselves. By discovering and owning your unique superpower you are able to powerfully step into your mission. Today Isabel Hundt is a successful Inspirational Speaker, Founder of the #ISeeUMovement, Sociologist, certified Transformation Coach working with Highly Sensitive Visionaries and World Changers aka Empath-Warriors™, Emotions Clearing Practitioner, published Author of The Power of Faith-Driven Success and 2x Amazon Bestselling Co-Author. Isabel obtained her degree in Sociology/Psychology at the University of Siegen in Germany and continues to be a student of life daily. Her expertise revolves around navigating your emotional world, the power of intuition and the importance of trust and perseverance in today's society. Isabel has been featured on over 100 TV shows, well-known radio and podcast shows.

London:

Claude Silver, Kevin Monroe

Garry Turner: Creating & facilitating the safe spaces that support unleashing people's innate brilliance

A game-changing thinker who develops strategies as to how to bring that thinking to life and implementation of the resulting solution. This has been evidenced throughout my career and more recently by leading, with support, human-centered projects such an in-house L&D project 'by the people for the people' saving £100k over 2 years vs external provision & a cultural team transformation resulting in > 40% additions in both sales and margin terms, by designing work around and unleashing the potential of people. – Keynote speaker on inter-departmental partnerships and the power of vulnerability – Enthusiastic human-centered solution provider across design, leadership & learning. Particular areas of focus include:– Cultural development (design & workshops)– Sales development (design & workshops)– Leadership safe spaces– Mindset– Trust– Curiosity– Wellbeing– Listening– Purpose & Values– Inclusion– Passionate about connecting human beings to one another that can serve the greater good– International sales & marketing professional with a deep-seated passion for driving optimum results through & not in spite of people.

Duena Blomstrom: Author, Keynote Speaker, Co-Founder and CEO of PeopleNotTech and Emotional Banking™

Duena is the author of the book "Emotional Banking: Fixing Culture, Leveraging FinTech and Transforming Retail Banks into Brands". She is a serial entrepreneur and intrapreneur, a mentor for start-ups, a LinkedIn Top Voice, named an industry influencer in most lists, a Forbes contributor, a blogger with cutting-edge, unconventional and unapologetic opinion style, an international keynote speaker at industry events, the inventor of the EmotionalBanking™ and MoneyMoments concepts and the Co-Founder and CEO of PeopleNotTech Ltd – a software solution provider revolutionizing the organizations of companies that need to use technology and new ways of work.

Rebecca-Monique Williams: Business and Personal Coach

Before recently embarking on a new professional venture as a Business and Personal Coach, Rebecca-Monique acquired over ten years of PeopleOps experience – in stand-alone roles and leading small teams in VC-backed tech start-ups – where she built out and scaled People functions from scratch to support plans for hyper growth. During her career as a People leader she was responsible for collaboratively designing, implementing and iterating holistic people-first processes, frameworks, guides and experiences spanning the entire employee lifecycle; including hiring, onboarding, and the growth & development of individuals and teams. Following weeks of introspection, Rebecca-Monique discovered that her role left her a few too many steps removed from fulfilling her professional purpose of directly enabling individuals to actualise their unique potential, so she decided to pursue coaching in a full-time capacity. Rebecca-

Monique delivers training and services to businesses that champion and foster the benefits a coaching organisation. She also coaches private clients in areas such as enhancing emotional intelligence, building confidence, and overcoming grief. "I am me, and you are you; respectively, that is our superpower....In order to truly coach, we must hold individuals with 'unconditional positive regard', listen to understand, and ask generative questions to unlock new thinking. There's a saying that if you want to explore anything in life, one must first look to the origin. I'm curious about people's values, needs, and motivations and wants; the stuff at the core, but sometimes beneath the surface. I provide that psychologically safe space for individuals to bring their authentic selves, and together we can explore a plethora of possibilities. It's my hope that after every interaction, they develop a greater sense of mobility to tackle their personal and professional challenges head on, and see those challenges not as problems, but as puzzles."

Special Thanks to sponsors and hosts of HumansFirst Club: Kristy McCann Flynn, GoCoach, Microsoft, Essilor, Arrow Electronics, Incubator/Chattanooga, Josh Newton, Newton Institute, IUPUI/Indianapolis, and Gavriella Shuster for their support.